I Will Be Your Voice

Your wings were ready,
but my heart was not

Claire Bodle

Copyright © 2025 Claire Bodle
Images Copyright © 2025 Claire Bodle

All rights reserved. No part of this publication may be reproduced, distributed or transmitted in any form or by any means, without prior written permission.

Disclaimer

This is a true story memoir, based on the author's personal memories and experiences. While every effort has been made to accurately depict the events as they occurred, the author acknowledges that memory can be subjective, and some details may have been altered or reconstructed to the best of her recollection.

The characters and events portrayed are based on real people and situations, and real names have been used with the intent to remain faithful to the truth of the author's experience. However, certain names, identifying details, or locations may have been changed to protect the privacy of individuals or to address concerns of confidentiality, where necessary.

Any resemblance to actual persons, living or dead, is unintended, except where specifically noted.

The publisher bears **no responsibility** for the content of this memoir or for any consequences arising from the publication, distribution, or reading of this book. The author assumes full responsibility and liability for any and all legal, emotional, financial, or social consequences that may arise from the story or its contents, including any potential grievances or remorse expressed by individuals mentioned in the book.

All liability of any kind, whether direct or indirect, is entirely the responsibility of the author.

This work reflects the author's personal perspective and interpretation of events, and the views expressed within are solely those of the author.

Cover Art © 2025 Lisa Williams Creativeify Studio
https://www.etsy.com/shop/CreativeifyStudio

I Will Be Your Voice: Your Wings Were Ready, But My Heart Was Not/ Claire Bodle

ISBN SC 978-1-7636700-1-3

In loving memory and dedicated to the love of my life,

my best friend,

my soulmate,

Richard.

CONTENTS

Chapter 1 1

Chapter 2 29

Chapter 3 41

Chapter 4 57

Chapter 5 67

Chapter 6 83

Chapter 7 99

Chapter 8 113

Chapter 9 131

Chapter 10 145

Chapter 11 157

Chapter 12 167

Chapter 13 173

Chapter One

The End

The phone rang at 4 a.m. on Wednesday the 13th of March, 2013. In that split second, everything changed. Our lives were thrown into an unthinkable and unbelievable chain of events that would never settle back to what it once was.

Richard was 13 days into his life-saving, life changing bone marrow transplant, and we had all been so hopeful for the future. We thought we were prepared for the tough road ahead, but nothing could have prepared us for what was about to come.

The voice on the other end of the phone belonged to an ICU registrar. His tone was measured, but the gravity of his words hit me like a ton of bricks.

"Mrs Bodle?" he asked, his voice cutting through the stillness of the early morning.

"Yes?" I responded, my heart was already beginning to race.

"I'm calling about Richard. There has been a sudden and very serious decline in his condition. He is on life support in the ICU. I am afraid he is extremely unwell. You need to come to the hospital straight away. How long do you think you will be?"

I froze, the words not sinking in, as if they had been spoken in a foreign language. Just 12 hours earlier, I had walked Richard to the bathroom in his single room in the bone marrow transplant unit. He was unwell, yes, but we had been reassured time and time again that it was "normal post-bone marrow transplant sick." The doctors had told us that what Richard was feeling and experiencing was to be expected, a part of the process.

It wasn't supposed to end like this.

In that moment, I felt like I was outside my own body, watching from a distance as this nightmare unfolded. I couldn't grasp what was happening—how had everything gone so terribly wrong in just a few short hours? My mind was racing, trying to catch up with the reality of what the ICU Registrar had just told me.

I couldn't stop shaking. Shock had gripped my entire body, and the room seemed to spin around me. It wasn't long before Emily and Nicholas, our eldest two, stirred from their sleep. They must have sensed something was very wrong. I could see the worry and concern etched on their faces as they looked at me, their eyes wide with fear and confusion. I tried to hold it together for their sake, but I was falling apart inside.

I needed to get to the hospital—there was no question about that. But the Hospital in Sydney was an hour away, and we were on the Central Coast. Driving there was not an option, I could barely think straight, let alone navigate the motorway in the dark in the state I was in. I felt utterly helpless, desperate to be by Richard's side but paralysed by the enormity of what I had just been told.

In a panic, I grabbed my phone and started calling my sisters. I needed someone, anyone, to help me. I rang them all, over and over again, knowing it was a long shot given the hour, but praying someone would answer. The silence on the other end of every phone call only made my anxiety worse. Finally, after what felt like an eternity, Victoria, my youngest sister, picked up.

I could barely get the words out. My voice was shaky, and I was trying so hard not to completely break down. "Victoria... it's Richard... he's on life support in ICU, I need to get to the hospital. I can't drive. I can't do this."

Victoria didn't hesitate. She was at a health retreat in the Hunter Valley, a good distance away, but said she would leave immediately to come and get me. I could hear her already moving about, packing up her things as she reassured me that she was on her way.

As I hung up the phone, a small sense of relief washed over me—Victoria was coming, and I wouldn't have to face this alone. But the clock was ticking, and every minute felt like an eternity. I looked over at Emily and Nicholas, who were sitting together on our bed, their eyes still fixed on me, waiting for answers I didn't have.

I took a deep breath, trying to steady myself. "Aunty Victoria is coming to take me to the hospital," I told them, my voice trembling. "Dad is really, really sick."

They nodded, trying to be brave, but I could see the fear in their eyes. I wanted to comfort them, to tell them that everything would be alright, but I couldn't bring myself to say those words. Not when I wasn't sure if they were true.

Victoria arrived at our house about an hour later. By this time my oldest sister Sally had returned my call and was on her way to our house as well. I left Emily, Nicholas and Zach at home pending Sally's imminent arrival and went to the hospital with Victoria.

We arrived at the hospital at around 6:30 a.m., my heart pounding in my chest as Victoria and I made our way straight to the ICU. The sterile smell of the hospital, the harsh fluorescent lights, and the quiet murmur of activity in the corridors all felt surreal, as if I were in a dream I couldn't wake up from.

As we reached the ICU reception, the Registrar was paged. He appeared quickly, his expression serious, his manner calm but heavy with the weight of what he was about to say. I could feel the tension in the air, my stomach twisting in knots as I tried to prepare myself for whatever he was about to tell me.

He gently guided us to a quiet corner, away from the bustle of the unit, and asked me to sit down. His eyes were full of empathy, but his tone was matter-of-fact, the kind of tone that doctors use when they are delivering the most difficult of news.

"Before you go in to see Richard, I need to talk to you about his condition," he began, his voice steady but low. "He is extremely unwell, and we are doing everything we possibly can to keep him alive. We have maxed out all the medical support we can give him at this time."

I felt a lump forming in my throat, but I forced myself to listen, to understand what he was saying. The reality of the situation was hitting me like a tsunami, but I knew I had to stay strong, to absorb every word, even though I desperately didn't want to hear them. I just wanted to completely break down, cry and fall apart.

He then asked, "How far away are your children?"

I swallowed hard, trying to keep my voice from shaking. "Just over hour," I replied, knowing full well that with peak hour traffic, it could take even longer.

He paused for a moment, his face clouded with concern. "I don't know if we can keep him alive for that long," he said quietly, his words like a knife through my heart.

I felt the world crumble beneath me. The thought of our children not getting the chance to say goodbye to their father was so overwhelming and too much to bear.

The registrar led me down the stark corridor towards Richard's room. Even now, 12 years later, I can still remember every sensory detail of that ICU room. The sharp antiseptic smell mixed with the subtle undertone of medical-grade plastic, the soft yet incessant beeping of monitors and machines, the low hum of the ventilator—it was a symphony of sounds, sights and scents that has been etched permanently into my memory.

As I entered, the cold fluorescent lights cast a harsh glow over the room, illuminating Richard lying there, connected to a web of tubes and machines. But what struck me most was how out of place he looked amidst all the medical paraphernalia. He didn't look like a man on the brink of death. Far from it.

Richard was a tall, strong, and an undeniably fit man. Just weeks prior, he was at the gym three times a week, pushing weights and running on the treadmill. On weekends, you'd find him carving up the waves at our favourite surf spots along the Central Coast with family and friends. His tanned skin, toned muscles, and the broadest of shoulders were a picture of health and vitality.

Yet here he was, lying motionless in a drug-induced coma, life support machines doing the breathing for him. His chest rose and fell rhythmically, but not of his own accord. The sight was jarring, a cruel juxtaposition that my mind struggled to reconcile. How could someone so full of life be now teetering on its edge?

I approached his bedside, my legs feeling like lead. Reaching out, I took his hand—still warm, still familiar. His face was serene, almost as if he was just in a deep sleep. For a fleeting moment, I allowed myself the fantasy that he'd open his eyes, and everything would be ok. But he didn't and he wasn't going to. Reality crashed down on me, heavier than ever.

My brain was refusing to process it. The image before me clashed violently with every memory I had of Richard. This was the man who'd chase the kids around the backyard, who'd dive into the ocean with reckless abandon, who'd dance with me under the stars on our anniversaries. Now, he lay silent, machines keeping him tethered to this world.

Tears blurred my vision as I leaned in closer, whispering words of love and encouragement, hoping that he could hear me, and that somewhere deep within, he would find the strength to fight, to stay with me, with us. The weight of my whole world now pressed down on me, making it hard to breathe.

Outside, the world continued its relentless march forward. The morning sun would be rising over Sydney, casting its golden hues over the Harbour Bridge and waking the city from its slumber. Commuters would be grumbling about traffic, baristas would be brewing the first coffees of the day, and life, in all its mundane glory, would go on.

But in that ICU room, time stood still. All that existed was Richard and the faint hope I desperately held on to that he would pull through this. The rest of the world faded into insignificance as I sat there, holding his hand, praying for a miracle.

Victoria had taken it upon herself to call Richard's mum, Doreen. She explained, with as much care and love as she could, that Richard's condition had taken a sudden and very severe decline for the worse and he had been put on life support. Doreen needed to get to the hospital as soon as possible. I could only imagine how that phone call must have hit her—a mother being told that her son, her strong, vibrant son, was now fighting for his life. I knew she'd be on her way, battling her own storm of emotions as she made the journey from the Northern Beaches.

By this time my sister Sally had arrived at the hospital, it was around 9 a.m. She had our three children with her— Emily 19, Nicholas 17 and Zach, just 10 years old. As they walked through the hospital doors, the weight of what they were about to face hung so heavily on me. I saw them before they saw me, their faces pale, eyes wide with a mixture of fear and disbelief. My heart shattered seeing them like that, knowing that they were about to confront the unimaginable.

We gathered just outside Richard's room, and I tried to prepare them, but how do you prepare your children for something like this? There are no words, no reassurances that can soften the blow of seeing their dad, the man who had been their protector, their hero, lying there so fragile, so vulnerable, so lifeless.

As we stepped into the room together, the air seemed to thicken with an unbearable tension. The kids were silent, their footsteps hesitant as they approached the bed. The sight of Richard hooked up to all those machines was soul destroying. Emily clutched my arm, her eyes brimming with tears, while Nicholas stood frozen, his usual confidence crumbling, and little Zach, our baby, looked up at me, his expression a heartbreaking mix of confusion and fear. He was too young to fully understand, but old enough to sense that something was terribly wrong.

There are no words or emotions in this world that can truly capture what they felt in that moment, seeing their dad for the first time on life support. The shock, the pain, the overwhelming helplessness and disbelief was all written on their faces. Emily's tears spilled over, and she let out a soft anguished sob. Nicholas, trying so hard to be strong, but the unstoppable tears flowed. Zach reached out to touch his dad's hand, his small fingers trembling as they wrapped around Richard's.

I stood beside them, holding them close, trying to offer comfort even as I was breaking apart inside. I wanted to shield them from this, to protect them from the cruelty of what was happening, but there was no escape. All I could do was be there with them, to share in their pain, to let them know that they weren't alone.

The room was quiet, filled with the steady, rhythmic sounds of machines, a harsh reminder of the thin thread that was keeping Richard with us. It was a sound that would stay with us forever, a haunting echo of the most difficult day of our lives. Our kids stood there, their tears falling freely now, as they took in the sight of their dad—so strong in their memories, yet so fragile and still before them.

We all knew, even without saying it, that time was seemingly running out. In that moment, I knew what I had to do. The enormity of it settled heavily on my shoulders, but there was no other way, no other option. I decided that I would be the one to tell our children the heartbreaking truth—that their dad was going to die. It was a decision of raw love and the fierce need to protect them from the cold, clinical delivery of that news from a stranger, even if that stranger was a doctor or the specialist who had known and looked after Richard for 21 years.

The doctors had been brutally honest with me about Richard's condition. They didn't sugarcoat it, and deep down, I knew I couldn't afford to either. Time was slipping through our fingers, and there was no room for false hope or softened truths. I had to step up, no matter how much it tore me apart inside.

I took our children outside Richard's room, held them close, my voice trembling but steady as I began to speak. "I need to tell you something," I started, trying to keep my own emotions in check, but failing miserably. "Dad is very, very sick. The doctors have done everything they can, but they don't think they can keep him alive for much longer. He is going to die."

Saying those words felt like a betrayal, like I was somehow giving up on Richard by speaking them out loud. I hated every syllable as it left my mouth. I hated that this was the reality we were facing, and I hated myself for being the one to shatter their world with that devastating truth. But I knew it had to be said. They deserved to hear it from me, from someone who loved them and understood the pain that those words would bring.

The room fell into a heavy silence, the weight of my words sinking in. And then, as if the dam had broken, our tears cascaded, the sound of our undeniable love and heartache for Richard, for their dad, I can still hear and feel to this day.

Richard's mum, Doreen, was beside herself with grief. Her sobs echoed through the room, raw and unfiltered, a mother's heart breaking as she watched her son slipping away. The sound was almost too much to bear, a visceral expression of the pain that we were all feeling but couldn't fully articulate.

I stood there, holding our children as they cried, feeling their pain which parallelled my own. Richard lay there, surrounded by machines, drips, and tubes, the very things keeping him alive, if only just. The mechanical beeping of the monitors, the rhythmic hiss of the ventilator, the cold sterility of the ICU—everything about it felt so wrong, so out of place for a man who had lived his life with such genuine passion and love for his family, friends and faith with all-encompassing reality and depth.

I can still hear those cries, the aching sobs, those sounds etched deep into my soul. It's a sound that will never leave me, a haunting reminder of that day, of those hours. The grief in that room was palpable, a heavy, suffocating presence that seemed to press down on all of us. We were powerless in the face of it, caught in an unbelievable, snowballing chain of events that none of us could stop.

In that moment, I wanted nothing more than to shield my children, to take away their pain, but all I could do was hold them close and let them cry. Our reality was unbearable, but we had no choice but to face it together, as a family.

At one point, one of the ICU doctors came into Richard's room, checking on his vitals and the machines that hummed softly in the background, each sound a reminder of how desperate and sad our world had become. As the doctor made his rounds, Richard's mum, Doreen, broke down completely. Through her tears, she pleaded with the doctor, her voice trembling with raw desperation.

"Please, take my life instead. Spare him, please, just take me," she begged, her hands reaching out as if she could somehow trade places with her son. It was the plea of a mother who would have done anything, given anything, to save her son. The doctor, compassionate but helpless, gently shook his head, his own eyes reflecting the sorrow of a situation where all the knowledge and skill in the world couldn't change the inevitable.

Before long, the small room just outside had filled with family, each person arriving with a look of shock and sorrow. Richard's sister, Joanne, who also lived on the Northern Beaches, was among the first to arrive. She rushed into the room, her disbelief and overwhelming sadness evident.

All three of my sisters were now there too—Victoria, who had brought me to the hospital, Sally, who had driven our kids down, and Kathryn, who had arrived shortly after. The small ICU room was crowded with grief, a family united by love but shattered by the gravity of the unfolding weight of unstoppable impending loss.

Meanwhile, Richard's oldest sister, Diane, and her husband, Kerry, were holidaying in Adelaide, frantically trying to arrange an emergency flight to Sydney. The distance between them and Richard felt a world away, a cruel barrier keeping them from being by his side. They were on the phone constantly, battling with airlines and travel arrangements, desperate to get to the hospital before it was too late.

And then there was Richard's twin sister, who lived in New Zealand with her family. The bond between them was special, as only twins can have, and the news of Richard's condition had obviously and without doubt devastated her. She too was scrambling to find an emergency flight over, the ocean between them now feeling like an insurmountable obstacle. I could only imagine the emotional turmoil and distress she was going through, of being so far away when time was not on our side.

The hospital waiting room was filling with enormously worried family and friends all doing what they could to get to Richard. Phones rang endlessly, with updates and frantic attempts to find flights and arrange travel continued. There was an urgency in the air, a collective desperation to reach

Richard in time, to say goodbye, to hold his hand, to tell him they loved him.

In the midst of it all, I felt a strange numbness settle over me, a sort of autopilot taking over as I moved between our children, Doreen, and the other family members. The room was a blur of faces, of tears and hushed conversations, but my focus remained on Richard. He was the reason we were all there, and my heart ached knowing that these might be the final moments we would have with him.

The minutes ticked by, each one feeling like an eternity, yet also slipping away so quickly. There was nothing more to do but wait, surrounded by the love and support of our family, our friends, all of us holding onto each other as we navigated the darkest hours of our lives.

Our son, Nicholas, had been incredibly strong throughout this whole ordeal. He had already given so much to his dad, literally a part of himself, when he became Richard's bone marrow donor. Now, in what felt like a last, desperate bid to save Richard, the doctors decided to try one final procedure. They took Nicholas away to the same part of the hospital where, not long ago, they had harvested his bone marrow. This time, they were going to syphon off his white blood cells, hoping to infuse them back into Richard to give him every possible chance to fight the raging infection that was coursing through his veins and already weakened body.

Victoria went with Nicholas, her presence a source of comfort in an otherwise terrifying situation. I knew Nicholas must have been feeling overwhelmed, not just physically but emotionally too. He was just 17, yet here he was, being asked to do something so monumental, something that carried the weight of his dad's life on his shoulders. I couldn't be with him in that moment, but I prayed that he knew how proud I was of him, how much I loved him, and how much his courage meant to all of us.

As Nicholas was prepped and connected to the blood filtering machine, I imagined him lying there, trying to be strong, trying to focus on the hope that this procedure might just be the miracle we needed. The doctors and nurses moved with quiet efficiency, their faces a mix of determination and concern. They were doing everything they could, pushing the limits of medical science and knowledge, to give Richard every fighting chance.

Back in the ICU, the atmosphere was a blend of hope and despair. The incomprehensible presumption of Richard's inevitable death continued to hang over us like a dark heavy cloud, but the medical team wasn't giving up. Despite the odds, they were pouring every ounce of their expertise, every possible resource, into keeping him alive. It was a battle against time, against the relentless progression of the infection, against the fragile balance of life and death.

I watched as the nurses checked the machines, adjusted the medications, and monitored Richard's vital signs with unwavering focus. The doctors consulted with each other in hushed tones, discussing the next steps, considering every option, no matter how slim the chances. There was no giving up, not yet. They knew, as we all did, that this might be our last hope, and they were determined to do everything within their power to possibly save him.

Even in the midst of this nightmare, I found a small measure of solace in the knowledge that Nicholas's sacrifice wasn't in vain. The procedure wasn't just a medical intervention—it was a symbol of the love and bond between father and son. Nicholas was doing everything he could to save his dad, and the doctors were doing everything they could to make that possible.

As I sat by Richard's side, holding his hand, crying, praying, pleading for a miracle and watching the machines literally keeping him alive, I clung to that glimmer of hope. The doctors were still fighting, and so were we. Despite everything, despite the overwhelming odds and the unbearable weight of uncertainty, we were not ready to give up, not ready to let go. Not yet.

Later that day, more people who loved Richard began to arrive, each bringing with them memories, love, and a deep sense of connection. Richard's childhood friend, Jamie, walked into the ICU with his wife, Annie, by his side. Jamie and Richard had been childhood friends for as long as I could remember, their bond forged over decades of growing up together, playing soccer, and going on family holidays. Seeing Jamie there, his face apparent with worry and sadness, was both comforting and heart-wrenching. He had always been there for Richard, and now, in the most difficult of times, he was here again.

Not long after, one of Richard's surfing buddies, joined us as well. The sight of him normally so full of life and energy, now subdued and struggling to hold back tears, was another stark reminder of how much Richard meant to everyone who knew him. The friends that had once shared their love of surfing were now gathered around Richard in this sterile hospital room, united by a love that transcended words.

The room was filled with so much love and emotion, a potent mix of disbelief and agonising hope. We all wanted so desperately for some miracle; some sign that Richard could pull through this. But with every update from the doctors—each one more discouraging than the last—it became harder and harder to hold onto that hope. It was as if the walls were literally closing in, and reality was becoming undeniably apparent.

I didn't know how to do this. I didn't know how to let our children watch their dad, their hero, slip away. How was I supposed to help them navigate this? How was I supposed to stand there and watch the man I loved more than anything in this world, the father of our children, die? Every instinct in me screamed to protect them, to shield them from this unbearable pain, but there was no way to stop it or prevent it.

I felt utterly lost, helpless against the relentless march of time. Richard's breaths, assisted by the machines, were becoming more laboured, and each one felt like a countdown, a ticking clock that I couldn't ignore. I wanted to reach out, to stop the inevitable, to hold him close and keep him here with us. But I knew, deep down, that this was a fight we were losing.

The love in that room was overwhelming, but so was the pain. We were all grappling with the same impossible questions: How do you say goodbye when you're not ready? How do you let go of someone who is so integral to your life, your family, your world? I didn't have any answers. I didn't know how to guide our children through this, or even how to guide myself.

All I could do was hold onto Richard's hand and hope that he felt our love, that he knew we were all there with him, surrounding him with everything we had. Even as the updates grew bleaker, as hope began to dim, I couldn't bring myself to let go. It wasn't just about losing Richard; it was about losing the life we had built together, the future we had dreamed of, and the heart of our family.

I wanted to believe and hoped that somehow, some way, Richard could hear us, that he knew we were all there, fighting alongside him. As the hours passed, so did the hope we were desperately clinging to. We were running out of time, and I didn't know how to face it. I didn't know how to say goodbye.

At approximately 12 p.m., Richard's specialist of 21 years took me aside. His expression was heavy with the burden of the news he was going to deliver, his eyes filled with a deep sadness and sorrow that mirrored my own. He was a man who had fought tirelessly alongside us, who had known Richard for the 21 years he had fought this cancer, and who had hoped, just as we all had, for a different outcome. As he spoke, his voice was soft, almost hesitant, as if he wished he could be saying anything else.

"We've isolated the source of the infection," he began, each word carefully chosen, there is nothing more we can do for him now, we have exhausted every possibility to be able to save his life. The finality of his words hung in the air between us, an unspoken echo of all the efforts that had been made, all the prayers that had been whispered, and all the hope that had been held onto for so long, albeit just 6 short hours.

He continued, gently explaining that the decision had been made to stop all treatment. Those words crashing down on me, a cold, crushing realization that this was it—

the end. I had known this moment was coming, but hearing it spoken out loud made it all too real. There was no more room for hope, no more waiting for a miracle. The fight was over.

As he spoke, I found myself looking at him not with anger or resentment, but with an overwhelming sense of sadness and empathy. He looked absolutely gutted, as though he was carrying the pain of this loss right alongside me. I could see how much this was affecting him, how much he had wanted to give us better news, to be the bearer of hope instead of despair. His compassion, his sorrow, was evident in every line of his face, and for a brief moment, my own grief was intertwined with a deep sense of sorrow for him—for the difficult role he had to play, for the weight of the words he had to deliver.

I felt an odd sense of responsibility to comfort him, even though I was the one who had just been given the most devastating news of my life. "Thank you," I managed to say, my voice trembling. It seemed absurd to thank him for something so heartbreaking, but I wanted him to know that I understood. I knew he and everyone else had done everything they could, that this was not just a loss for us, but for him too.

As he left me alone with my thoughts, I stood there, numb and disoriented. The realization of what was about to happen settled over me like a thick suffocating fog. How was

I going to tell our children? How was I going to gather the strength to face what came next? My mind raced with the enormity of it all, yet in that moment, all I could feel was a profound sadness and paralysing ache—for Richard, for our family, our friends and even his specialist who had just broken our hearts with his words.

The decision had been made. There was nothing left to fight for, nothing left to do but be there, to surround Richard with our love in his final moments. The room that had once been filled with hope and determination now fell silent and still, as if the very air had been drained of life. And yet, even in the depths of this despair, I knew we had to find a way to say goodbye.

The atmosphere outside Richard's ICU room was charged with an intense blend of love, disbelief, and sorrow. The Minister from our church had arrived, a comforting presence in the midst of our anguish. His arrival was a small but significant beacon of support and spiritual solace in our time of need. He moved among us, offering quiet prayers and words of comfort, trying to ease the heavy burden that none of us could understand or fathom.

In this moment, too, the medical team had decided to stop the process of extracting Nicholas's white blood cells. They understood how important it was for him to be with his dad in these final moments. Nicholas was brought back to us heartbroken. He returned to the ICU room, his face pale and drawn, but his eyes filled with tears and the same love that had driven him to donate his bone marrow in the first place.

The scene within the room was one of unbearable finality. The doctors and nurses worked with a quiet, almost reverent efficiency as they began to turn off all the drips, life-sustaining drugs, and machines that had been keeping Richard alive. Each click and hiss of the machines ceasing was another step closer to the end. It was a process so clinical and impersonal, so starkly contrasted with the deep personal pain and loss we were experiencing.

The ICU registrar approached me with a gentle, almost apologetic demeanor. "I don't think it will be too long now," she said softly. Her words were both a reassurance and pure fear of what was about to happen.

I took a deep breath, trying to slow every emotion down. The room was filled with an overwhelming silence, punctuated only by unimaginable soul-destroying crying and sobbing. Richard lay there, so still, his once strong and vibrant presence now a life and soul that was about to be so cruelly and so unfairly taken from us. I could barely bring myself to look at him, yet I couldn't look away. I wanted to remember him as he was before this all began, full of life, full of strength, full of hope.

Emily, Nicholas and Zach were at Richard's bedside. Holding his hand, touching his arm, speaking softly to him, and saying their final goodbyes. Emily's tears fell freely as she stroked his hair. Nicholas's strength broken as his tears also fell. Zach stood a solitary figure at the end of his dad's bed, scared with tears streaming down his little face, refusing to come any closer.

The Minister stood by, offering quiet prayers, his presence a comforting reminder that we were not alone in this. He spoke of peace and solace, of the promise of a life beyond this one, trying to offer us some measure of comfort amidst the profound sadness.

Minutes went by, each one feeling like an eternity. I lay on Richard's chest trying to hold onto every detail of him, to imprint the memory of his face and his presence in my heart. I wanted to be strong for the kids, to offer them comfort, but I couldn't, my heart and my world were shattering into thousands and thousands of pieces.

The room seemed to hold its breath as we waited, each of us grappling with our own thoughts and emotions. The reality of the situation was inescapable, and as the moments passed, the space around us felt charged with incredibly heavy, sad and quiet anticipation.

And then, in the stillness of that moment, I knew that the time was near. Richard's breaths grew shallower, more spaced out. The fight was over. The love we had for him, the hope we had clung to, and the painful acceptance of what was happening all condensed in those final moments.

We were whispering our final goodbyes to let him go with all the love we had in our hearts. It was the hardest thing I'd ever had to do, but it was the only thing left we had to give.

I lay my head on Richards still big strong chest. I could hear his heart beating. I didn't want to hear his heart stop beating, so I moved my head further onto the right side of his chest until it had faded. His chest, soaked wet from my tears, continued to rise and fall, the ventilator was still, unbeknownst to me, active.

Approximately 20 minutes later, the ICU Registrar entered the room with a sombre expression. She approached me gently, her eyes filled with the kind of compassion that only comes from shared grief. "I'm so sorry," she said softly. "Richard has passed away."

The room was filled with a profound silence as we absorbed those words. The machines that had once beeped and hummed now stood idle, a stark reminder of the life that had just slipped away. The once vibrant and strong man who had fought so valiantly was now at peace, but it was a peace that came at an unbearable cost.

I looked around at the faces of our children, at Nicholas, Emily, and Zach, who were still at their dad's side, their eyes swollen from crying. They had witnessed their father's final moments, and the depth of their grief was palpable. My heart ached for them, for their pain, and for the loss of their father's presence in their lives.

Richard's mum, Doreen, was clutching a tissue tightly, her shoulders shaking with quiet sobs. She had been there through it all, a rock of support for Richard and the family, and now she was facing the unimaginable pain of losing her son.

Our family and friends stood in sombre solidarity, their own grief mingling with ours. Our Minister continued to offer words of comfort, but the reality was that no words could truly alleviate or diminish anything we were feeling at all.

Richard's sister Diane and her husband Kerry arrived from Adelaide unfortunately just after he passed away. Thankfully, as we all did, they got a chance to say goodbye to Richard after they had removed all the tubes, drips and machines from him.

Richard's twin sister Sarah unfortunately couldn't get a flight that day and didn't make it to the hospital to say goodbye to her brother.

As the reality of Richard's passing began to sink in, I struggled to process the enormity of it. He had been a force of strength and love in our lives, a pillar of support and joy. Now, the void left by his absence felt insurmountable, a gaping wound in the fabric of our family.

In the quiet moments that followed, as the world outside continued on without knowing the depth of our loss, I found myself grappling with the impossibility of saying goodbye forever. The finality of it was overwhelming, unbearable and soul destroying. I felt a deep, aching sadness for the future that we would now have to navigate without him.

In the 13th hour of the of 13th day of the 3rd month of 2013, Richard lost his 21-year battle with Non-Hodgkin's Lymphoma. He was only 47 years old. The bone marrow transplant never had a chance to take.

This photo was given to me of the sunrise the day
Richard died by my beautiful friend, Mindy

Chapter Two

The Beginning

I met Richard when I was just turning 17 years old. That time is etched in my memory, mostly because of a funny little moment that has always stayed with me. Richard, in his thoughtful but occasionally overlooked attention to detail way, gave me a "Happy 18th Birthday" card that year, one whole year ahead of schedule! It was the first of many endearing "attention to detail… not" moments that became a hallmark of Richard's personality and never failed to make me laugh.

Our paths first crossed one day at a mutual friend's house. Greg, a friend of Richard's, was having a small get-together at his place. Richard, also one of Greg's mates from the neighbourhood, was invited along. I didn't know it then, but this chance encounter would be the beginning of a lifelong love story. Interestingly enough, Greg would make another surprising appearance later in our lives, but we'll get to that in due course.

Richard came from a close-knit family. He was one of four children, raised by Maurice and Doreen. He had two older sisters, Diane and Joanne, and a twin sister, Sarah. Their childhood was spent in Balgowlah Heights, on Sydney's Northern Beaches, a beautiful, sun-soaked place that held so many of Richard's cherished memories. Coincidentally, I grew up in the same area, though our lives didn't cross paths until that day at Greg's house.

I was the second of four daughters in my family. My parents, Russell and Margaret, raised me and my three sisters; Sally, Kathryn, and Victoria, right there in Balgowlah Heights on the Northern Beaches too. Life was busy in our households growing up, but little did I know that soon my world would intertwine with Richard's in ways that I couldn't yet imagine.

At just 19, Richard took a bold step and joined the New South Wales Police Force. He graduated from the Police Academy and was first deployed to King's Cross, one of the busiest and most intense areas in Sydney, for his first assignment. For the next 17 years, Richard worked his way up to a Senior Constable Police Officer, serving at several stations including Central, Mosman, Manly, Dee Why, Chatswood, and eventually Gosford on the NSW Central Coast. Policing was more than just a job for Richard, he was truly dedicated. He carried himself with a quiet confidence, and his natural sense of duty and care for others shone through in his work.

I followed a different path. I wanted to be a nurse, starting with a Diploma of Applied Science at Sydney College, which later merged with Sydney University. It was a fulfilling journey, one that allowed me to care for people in their most vulnerable moments. I graduated as a Registered Nurse, and now, 33 years later, I am still working as a Senior Surgical Registered Nurse. It's a career that has shaped me in so many ways, and I think Richard always admired the dedication we both had to helping others, him in law enforcement, and me in healthcare.

Our first date was a day I will never forget. Richard, being the adventurous type, took me sailing on his family's catamaran in Sydney Harbour. It was magical. We set out on a picture-perfect day, with the sun shining and a gentle breeze guiding us across the water. We sailed over to Watson's Bay, then onto Quarantine Beach, where we spent the afternoon swimming and sunbaking in the warm sun. It felt like something out of a movie, just us, the ocean, and the promise of something special on the horizon.

On the way back to Forty Baskets Beach, where we had started our date, Richard decided to inject a bit of excitement into the day. In what he thought was a hilarious move, he decided to 'play chicken' with the Manly Ferry, a massive passenger vessel that dwarfed our little catamaran.

Needless to say, it was not hilarious, at least not to me! As the ferry loomed closer, I remember yelling at him to stop mucking around, my heart racing as I clutched the sides of the boat. In true Richard fashion, he thought it was all in good fun and laughed it off, but that was one of the many moments that showed me just how daring he could be, always willing to push the boundaries, sometimes a little too far for my liking.

Still, it was impossible not to be charmed by him. There was something magnetic about Richard, a mix of strength, humour, and that occasional cheekiness that made him so unforgettable. That first date, despite the ferry scare, was the start of many more adventures we would share. In those early days, I already knew Richard was someone special. There was an ease in how we connected, and even as young as we were, I could feel that our lives were beginning to weave together in ways that would shape everything that came after.

When he dropped me home after that incredible yet slightly terrifying first date, I was buzzing with excitement, completely nervous, and over the moon! As I climbed out of the car, I tried to play it cool, winding up the window while saying my goodbyes. But in my giddy state, I hadn't realised that my long hair had somehow gotten caught in the window. Trying to walk away gracefully, thinking I looked sexy, I was yanked backwards with a jolt! The window had trapped my hair, and there I was, pulled back by my own mane, looking anything but elegant! It wasn't my finest moment, and certainly not the sexy exit I had envisioned. Still, Richard found it hilarious, and I couldn't help but laugh at the absurdity of it all.

Another date that stands out as a classic 'Richard moment' was a dinner at *Ribs and Rumps* in Manly. It was one of those fun, laid-back beachfront restaurants known for their massive portions. If you ordered the ribs, and naturally, we did, you were handed this comically large white paper bib to wear, a necessity for tackling the Flintstone-sized ribs we were served. We had managed to snag a window table and were happily tucking into our dinner, bibs and all, when Richard's attention was suddenly drawn to something outside.

He glanced out the window, his eyes locking onto a man walking by. "That's him! We've been looking for that bloke for ages. He's a wanted felon!" Richard said, mid-bite. I barely had time to process what he was saying before he leapt up from the table, leaving me sitting there alone, still holding my ribs. He quickly called for backup and stormed out to make the arrest, right there on the beachfront in full view of the restaurant.

I could see it all unfold through the window. Richard, now in full police mode, moving in to apprehend the man. It was a surreal sight, my date turned crime-fighter right before my eyes. But then I noticed something that made me wide eyed for an entirely different reason: Richard was still wearing his giant paper bib! I frantically tried to get his attention, gesturing wildly from the table until he finally looked back at me. When I caught his eye, I mouthed, "Your bib! You still have your bib on!"

It was an unforgettable moment. Richard, serious and professional, executing an arrest with a big white bib hanging around his neck. I couldn't stop laughing once it was all over, and to this day, it remains one of my favourite memories from our early days together. It was so quintessentially Richard; serious about his duty, but with a touch of unintentional humour that made everything he did so endearing.

During those years, we both attended All Saints Anglican Church in Balgowlah regularly. It was a foundation for us, something we leaned on as our relationship grew stronger. Our faith was real, solid, and sustaining, providing us with strength and comfort through some of the hardest, saddest, darkest and most challenging years that lay ahead. We made lifelong friends during this time, many of whom remain close to me to this day.

Richard and I dated for four years, but it wasn't all smooth sailing. We had our ups and downs like any couple, even going through a couple of 'conscious uncouplings' during that time. Looking back, those breaks were brief but necessary. We were both young, still figuring out who we were and what we wanted from life and each other. But every time we found our way back to one another, it was with a renewed sense of commitment and love. It just felt so right.

In 1990, Richard proposed to me, and the pure joy and excitement I felt were beyond words. I was absolutely over the moon, convinced that I was the luckiest girl in the world. My love for him was immeasurable, and I thought nothing could ever change that. Nothing could ever change us. We had the world ahead of us, and I was certain our future together would be filled with love, laughter, and endless possibilities.

We were married on the 29th of June, 1991. I was just 22, and Richard was 26. Originally, I had wanted a summer wedding in 1992. Visions of warm weather and sunny skies filled my mind. But my mum, for a thousand reasons, insisted that we marry in June of 1991. At first, I was disappointed to change that timeline I had envisaged, but in hindsight, that decision would prove to be more significant than I could have ever imagined.

That Christmas, 6 months after we were married, Richard confided something in me that absolutely shook me. He told me that if he had known what was coming, he would never have married me. He said it out of love, knowing what lay ahead would be incredibly hard, a burden he didn't want me to bear. What was coming would change our lives forever, but despite the weight of his words, I had no doubt, no hesitation, that we were meant to be together. We were meant to get married when we did, exactly when we did. I know this not only because it allowed me to walk beside him through the hardest battles of his life, but also because of the extraordinary life we built together during the time we had.

The date was set, and on that wintery morning, we exchanged our vows at All Saints Anglican Church. It was an 11am ceremony, followed by a beautiful reception at Akuna Bay on Pittwater, nestled in the Ku-ring-gai Chase National Park. The day was a perfect reflection of life, unexpected and unpredictable. It was sunny one minute, raining the next, with gusts of wind and chilly air. We joked that we had all four seasons in one day, but it didn't matter. None of it dampened the happiness we felt or the love that surrounded us.

After the wedding, we honeymooned in Fiji for two magical weeks, soaking in the sun, sand, and crystal-clear waters. It was the perfect escape, just the two of us, dreaming about the life we were about to build together. It felt like we had forever ahead of us, an exciting new chapter waiting to unfold.

And so, we returned home, eager to start our new and exciting lives together as husband and wife. Little did we know the challenges that awaited us would be greater than we ever could have imagined. But in those early days, there was only love, hope, happiness, and the promise of forever.

In October of 1991, Richard and I decided to go on a four-week holiday, driving up to the Sunshine Coast in Queensland and staying at seaside accommodation all the way up and back. We swam, we sunbaked, we snorkeled, we explored, we ate, we drank. Life was good.

On the way back, Richard started to get a bit of a cough. We thought nothing of it and picked up some cough medicine to help.

We returned home at the beginning of November, and both went back to our respective jobs - Richard at Mosman Police Station and me at St Vincents Private Hospital.

His cough persisted and he went to our GP for a check-up. He was put on a course of antibiotics, with a prescription for another course if need be.

He finished the first course and didn't seem to be getting any better. If anything, he was getting worse. He filled the script for the second course of antibiotics, and we hoped this would kill the bug responsible for the ever worsening and concerning cough, which was almost asthma like.

Richard finished the second course of antibiotics and was still no better. A painless lump had also now appeared on his neck.

He went back to the GP, and after a thorough examination, he was sent for a chest x-ray. Richard was given the x-ray and report to take back to his GP at his next appointment.

When he got home, I opened that seal on the back of that large yellow envelope that said, 'Confidential - Do Not Open' and pulled out the single sheet report. I had only been nursing for approximately 10 months at this time, and when I read the word 'mass', I literally couldn't compute why they were using that word in his report. I knew what 'mass' meant, but why were they using it in his report? Richard was 26 years old. It didn't make sense.

We both went to his GP appointment a few days later, with that large yellow envelope that I had ever so carefully resealed the 'Do Not Open' sticker on. Richard was given urgent letters of referral to a hematologist and a radiologist at a large public Sydney Hospital.

After a lot of blood tests, a bone marrow biopsy, scans, and specialist appointments, Richard was given the life-changing and devastating news that he had Non-Hodgkins Lymphoma, a blood cancer. That mass in his chest x-ray was the size of his fist, a malignant tumour that was now pressing on his trachea and starting to compromise his airway.

This all happened a week before Christmas 1991. We had been married for six months. We sat in the hematologist's consulting room in shock, in silent fear and completely overwhelmed with a hundred other emotions, and that was just the beginning.

Richard's hematologist explained to us that his treatment was going to be aggressive: six months of intensive chemotherapy and radiotherapy.

As if all of that wasn't enough, it was then explained that with the aggressive and intensive treatment Richard was about to undergo, the probability of him becoming infertile was very high. We literally went straight from the hematologist's rooms to the IVF clinic in the next building.

Richard was taken away, and I was left by myself in a long empty corridor. I was 22 and Richard was 26. My husband had just been told he had cancer and that we may now never be able to have any children.

I sat in that clinical, cold, long, empty corridor alone and cried.

Our Wedding Day 1991

Chapter Three

Our Journey

Richard's real battle began at the start of 1992. In January, he started an intensive course of intravenous chemotherapy, and for the next 12 weeks, this became our new reality. Every week, like clockwork, we'd head into the hospital for his four-hour chemo session. It was gruelling, to say the least. But on top of the chemotherapy, Richard was also prescribed high doses of corticosteroids, 250mg of Prednisone a day, for those who are familiar with the medical side of things, which he took for five days straight each week, with a two-day break from them on weekends.

You would think the break would offer some relief, but unfortunately, it didn't. Those two days without the steroids were brutal. Richard would start withdrawing from them, which threw up a whole new set of challenges. The physical toll was bad enough, but the psychological and emotional impact was just as hard to watch.

For 12 weeks, Richard endured the same pattern: withdrawal symptoms, crushing fatigue, muscle and joint pain, nausea, vomiting and involuntary mood swings. Every week, as we drove home from the hospital, I'd brace myself for the storm that was about to hit; his body weakening more and more each week, and the chemo nausea and vomiting getting worse, despite the anti-nausea medication they gave him.

One memory, in particular, still haunts me. It was one of those low moments, the kind that stays with you forever. Richard was lying on the bathroom floor, his body overwhelmed with all consuming nausea. He was vomiting so violently he couldn't even lift his head. He just lay there vomiting over the drain, utterly defeated. I sat next to him on the cold tiles, feeling completely helpless. There was nothing I could do to stop it. I remember wiping his face with a cold wet towel, praying for it to end, for anything to make him feel better. I just wanted him to have a break from the endless suffering. But all I could do was sit there with him, being present, even though it felt like such a completely inadequate response to what he was going through.

By week six, Richard's hair had almost all fallen out. I remember watching him look at himself in the mirror, the frustration in his eyes. He didn't recognise the man staring back at him, and honestly, neither did I. This strong, vibrant man I had married was being reduced to a shadow of his former self, and it was happening right in front of him, of me. It was heartbreaking.

Work was out of the question for Richard by that stage. He was officially on leave, and thank God for that. He was so weak and exhausted that all he could manage was to sleep, rest, and then sleep some more. There were days when even getting out of bed seemed like an impossible task. He needed every bit of that time off to try and recover from each round of chemo.

Those three months were, without a doubt, some of the hardest of our lives. The toll it took on Richard, both physically and emotionally, was immense. I watched him go from being my strong, fit husband to someone who could barely muster the energy and strength to get through a day. It broke his spirit, and truthfully, it broke mine too. Watching the person you love more than anything in the world go through that level of suffering. It's indescribable.

Chemotherapy was meant to be his hope for a future, but instead, it felt like a never-ending nightmare. Hour after hour, day after day, week after week.

After Richard's 12 weeks of chemotherapy came to an end, we rolled straight into another 12 weeks of weekly radiotherapy. By then, he was absolutely drained, both physically and emotionally. But we made a decision that gave us something to hang onto and something to work towards. When all of his treatment was finished, when his body had time to heal, recover and he was feeling stronger, we were going to treat ourselves to a holiday, a big holiday to Europe and the UK.

This plan became a real game changer for us, especially for Richard. It wasn't just the thought of getting away, it was the idea that there was life after cancer and treatment, something to look forward to beyond the hospital walls and endless appointments. It became an amazing goal to work towards, a light at the end of a very dark tunnel.

Before starting radiotherapy, Richard had to be 'mapped.' This meant more scans and then marking the exact spots for the radiation with tiny dot tattoos. These little dots became permanent reminders of what he was enduring. Once the mapping was done, he got stuck into the radiotherapy sessions. Unlike chemo, radiotherapy wasn't as physically draining, but it still took its toll.

Richard started easing back into work while going through this treatment, which was something he desperately needed, not just for the routine but to feel like he was still part of the world outside of cancer. They put him on light duties at the front desk of the police station, which turned out to be perfect in an unexpected way. Richard was tall, solidly built, and now completely bald, which was an intimidating combination. The other officers loved it because his presence alone was enough to stop any troublemakers in their tracks. It gave him a bit of a laugh too, which was something we both sorely needed.

He completed his six months of treatment in the middle of winter. By then, we were practically counting down the days until our trip in October and November. We couldn't wait to get away, to escape from the constant pressure and fear that had been looming over us for so long. One of the highlights of our trip was going to be catching up with one of Richard's schoolmates who had moved to England with his wife. The thought of being somewhere far away, surrounded by old friends and new experiences, was so very much anticipated.

And then came the news we'd been praying for. Richard was officially in remission. It felt like the weight of the world had been lifted off our young shoulders. For the first time in a long time, we could actually breathe again. We were so ready to leave cancer behind, at least for a little while, and throw ourselves into living life.

That trip turned out to be everything we'd hoped for and more. We travelled for six blissful weeks, wandering through new countries, exploring different cultures, meeting incredible people, and simply enjoying the freedom of being alive and well. For the first time in what felt like forever, we could forget about the cancer, the endless treatments, and all the uncertainty and suffering.

We laughed, we relaxed, we lived. It was exactly what we needed.

Before we left, Richard's doctors had given us a bit of hope to cling to: if he stayed in remission for five years, the likelihood of the cancer returning would be slim. Those words became our lifeline. We clung to them with everything we had, holding onto the hope that this nightmare was finally behind us. It was fragile hope, the kind that almost hurts to hold onto because you're so scared of it slipping away. But we needed to believe it, to trust that the worst was over and that brighter days lay ahead.

In December 1992, a little miracle happened that we never saw coming. We found out I was pregnant. After being told that this would likely never happen naturally after the intense chemotherapy treatment Richard had endured. It felt like the world had tilted a little on its axis towards us. We were surprised, shocked, beyond thankful, and just over the moon. It was one of those moments where you can't believe it's real. This was the baby we had convinced ourselves that we thought we might never be able to have.

From the second I knew I was incredibly careful. Every step I took, every decision I made was about protecting that tiny life growing inside me. It felt too precious, too fragile, like the most important gift we could ever receive. The morning sickness kicked in hard, and honestly, it was brutal. I was sick all day and all night, but I didn't care in the slightest. We were having a baby, and that was all that mattered.

We hit the magical 12-week mark without any issues, and I can't describe the relief we felt. We could finally start telling people our exciting news; our family, friends, everyone who had been walking alongside us through such a tough journey. That feeling of pure joy and excitement was like a balm, softening the rough edges of the difficult path we'd been on since we got married. For the first time in a long while, things felt like they were turning around.

But life has a cruel way of throwing curveballs. At 15 weeks, I started bleeding. Panic gripped me instantly. We rushed in for an urgent ultrasound, hearts pounding, hoping for the best, but fearing the worst. As soon as the sonographer's face fell, I knew. The silence in that room was deafening. There was no heartbeat. Our little miracle baby, the one we had so badly wanted and hoped for, was gone.

The grief that followed was unbearably sad. It was as if the ground had been pulled out from under us. After everything we'd already been through, this loss felt particularly cruel. It was such a dark time, and trying to come to terms with it was like an impossible task. I didn't know how to make sense of the joy we'd felt, only for it to be so quickly ripped away.

Then, just a few months later in May 1993, another shock. We found out I was pregnant again, naturally, and completely unexpected. This time though, I didn't feel the same unbridled excitement. Instead, I was absolutely terrified. Every day felt like walking on a tightrope, balancing fear and hope, wondering if it would all come crashing down again. The idea of losing another baby, going through that grief again, was emotionally crippling. No matter how careful I was or how 'right' I tried to do everything, I couldn't shake the anxiety.

There was constant fear hanging over me, and while I tried to stay positive and hopeful, it was hard to shake the memories of what we'd already lost. This pregnancy felt different, not just because of the previous loss, but because now it was overshadowed by an almost paralysing sense of dread. All we wanted was for this little life to make it, for the miracle we had so desperately dreamed of to finally become a reality.

Wanting something with all your heart can be the most powerful force in the world, but sometimes, heartbreakingly, it's just not enough. This was a lesson we had to learn more than once as we navigated our life together. Every time we thought we had it figured out, life would sometimes have very different ideas.

When we got to the 12-week mark again in this pregnancy, the relief was overwhelming. I remember the ultrasound at eight weeks like it was yesterday, the tiny baby bouncing around inside me like it was having the time of its life in some kind of personal jumping castle. I was ecstatic. As much as I tried to relax and enjoy it, there was always that niggling worry in the back of my mind. Honestly, if I could have had an ultrasound every single day just for peace of mind, I would have.

By the time we hit 15 weeks, everything seemed to be progressing well. I was sick all the time, morning, noon, and night, vomiting on my way to work, vomiting during my shifts, and vomiting on the drive home. But you know what? I didn't care. Not one bit. As long as our baby was healthy, I would have happily thrown up every day for the rest of the pregnancy.

Finally, at 20 weeks, the constant sickness started to ease up. I could actually enjoy being pregnant. It was such a relief to feel like myself again, and even more so to feel the baby growing inside me, bouncing around in my ever-expanding belly. Richard and I were on cloud nine. He was healthy, I was starting to feel better, and our excitement about meeting our baby, due on Australia Day, 26th January 1994, was through the roof.

By 28 weeks, though, a new concern started to creep in. My blood pressure began to rise, and it wasn't going away. At 30 weeks, the doctors decided it was time to step in, so I was put on two different blood pressure medications to try and manage it. I was worried, but the doctors reassured us that it was still within the 'normal pregnancy high' range. Still, that didn't stop the 'what ifs' from spinning around in my head.

Even though my blood pressure remained high, I clung to the fact that we were within safe parameters. Every appointment, every check-up felt like a small victory. We were inching closer to the finish line, and despite the bumps along the way, it finally felt like we were going to bring our little miracle life into our world. I finally let out the breath I hadn't realised I'd been holding all this time.

At 34 weeks, my blood pressure just wouldn't let up, and the doctors decided it was time to admit me to hospital for strict bed rest. I knew it was serious, but part of me also thought, "how hard can bed rest really be?" Turns out, it was harder than I expected. But I stuck it out, and a week later, they let me out early. Apparently, 'on good behaviour!'

Richard came to pick me up from the maternity ward in his full police uniform while he was on duty. I have to say, he was a bit of a hit with the other mums and nurses in the ward, all eyes on him as he walked in. I couldn't help but feel a little smug myself. Here was my hero in blue, whisking me away. To top it off, we left the hospital in a police car, and honestly, I secretly loved every minute of it!

But the excitement was short-lived. I only managed to last two days at home before my blood pressure spiked again, and back into hospital I went. Things quickly escalated, and by 35 weeks, I was being prepped for an emergency caesarean. The doctors didn't mince words. They told me I had developed pre-eclampsia, which meant they needed to deliver the baby as soon as possible.

On the 23rd of December 1993, our little Christmas miracle arrived, Emily Victoria Bodle. She was absolutely perfect, weighing just 4lbs 14oz (2.21kg). Even though she was tiny, she had a fighting spirit that shone through from the moment she was born. Emily was taken off straight to the special care nursery, while I was sent to ICU. It wasn't exactly the picture-perfect birth I had imagined, but we had our beautiful baby girl, and that was all that mattered.

Seeing Richard hold Emily for the first time was something I'll never forget. He looked at her like she was the most precious thing in the world. Despite all the drama leading up to her arrival, in that moment, everything felt right. Our journey to parenthood had been tough, but holding Emily made it all worth it.

Emily spent the first four weeks of her life in the special care nursery, tube-fed through her nose into her tiny tummy. It was hard leaving her there when I was discharged after seven days, but I made it my mission to express milk as often as possible and take it into the hospital to make sure she was getting the best start.

I syringed my breast milk through the tube in her tiny little nose as I held her skin to skin on me. I remember feeling this huge mix of emotions; relief that she was safe and well, but also frustration at not being able to take her home with us. Every day we were with her in the nursery, it was like a little victory when she showed signs of getting stronger.

Finally, after four weeks, before her actual due date, Emily was strong enough to come home. And so, we began our little family life, just the three of us, in what felt like a perfect bubble. It was such a joy having her at home, and it really felt like we could take on anything now that she was in our arms, safe and sound.

When Emily was about seven months old, I decided to go back to work, which meant Richard and I had to master the art of shift work parenting. I worked afternoon shifts from 2:30pm to 11pm, and Richard was still on varying police shifts. We would 'tag team' looking after her, lovingly passing her between us like a baton in a relay race. It wasn't always smooth, but somehow, we made it work.

One of those early shifts after I went back to work sticks out in my memory. I had carefully prepared a healthy dinner for Emily, labelling it and putting it front and center in the fridge so Richard wouldn't miss it. When I got home later that night, the house was peaceful, everyone asleep. To my surprise, Emily's dinner was still sitting there, untouched. The next morning, I asked Richard why he hadn't fed her the meal I made.

"I couldn't find it," he said, "so she had some of my Chinese takeaway instead, which she loved!"

I remember laughing and shaking my head. That was just us, parenting by teamwork, even if it was a bit chaotic at times. It wasn't always by the book, but we made it through, and Emily was no worse for it. Somehow, it just worked.

When Emily was about nine months old, one evening we decided to get takeaway for dinner one night. My sister Kathryn was over, and we all tucked in, but not long after, we all became violently ill with food poisoning. The next few days were rough. Richard and my sister gradually started to feel better, but I didn't. I was still vomiting, feeling worse than they did. I knew something wasn't right.

After a week of feeling like death, I decided to take a pregnancy test, not because I thought I was pregnant, but more to rule it out.

But to my absolute shock, it was positive! I was already seven weeks pregnant. We couldn't believe it. After all the struggles we had to bring Emily into the world, we were now blessed with another little miracle. We had been so happy with just one baby, and now we were going to have two! The joy and disbelief were overwhelming. Life had taken yet another unexpected but wonderful turn.

I continued dealing with the relentless food poisoning-turned-morning sickness until I hit the 20-week mark, much like I had with Emily. By now, I was somewhat of a pro at managing it, though that didn't make the vomiting any easier. I was counting down the days until I could stop feeling so awful and start enjoying the pregnancy.

On July 26, 1995, two weeks earlier than planned, Nicholas Richard Bodle made his grand entrance into the world. My blood pressure had once again caused problems towards the end, and we had to go in for another emergency caesarean. Nicholas was a healthy 8lbs 3oz, strong and perfect baby boy. We were overjoyed. After a few days in the hospital, we headed home, now a little family of four.

Life became busier with two little ones in the house, but it was the happiest kind of busy. We loved watching our family grow, seeing Emily embrace her new role as a big sister, and witnessing Nicholas settle into our routine. Richard was thriving in fatherhood, doting on both the kids, and finding ways to juggle his shift work with family life.

Meanwhile, Richard had been well since the end of his cancer treatment back in June 1992. He had regular scans and check-ups to ensure that his remission was holding strong. There was always that underlying fear, but we were cautiously optimistic. The big milestone, the five-year remission mark, was approaching. For us, that meant the world. If Richard could stay in remission for five years, the doctors told us, the likelihood of the cancer returning was slim. That was our greatest hope, and we clung to it.

When the five-year anniversary of his remission came around, we celebrated with overwhelming gratitude. There were tears, joy, and the quiet but heavy relief that maybe, just maybe, we were in the clear. We had made it! Our lives, which had been so uncertain for so long, now felt filled with promise and hope. We had two beautiful children, Richard was well, and life felt right again.

But then, just one month after reaching that all-important milestone, Richard started experiencing some right-sided abdominal pain. It wasn't anything dramatic at first, just a persistent ache that grew over a couple of days. Richard, never one to make a fuss, went to see a GP during his lunch break at work one day, thinking it was probably gallstones or something minor. The GP agreed and ordered an ultrasound to be sure.

But it wasn't gallstones.

Richard's cancer had come back. This time, it was in his abdomen. The news was unbearably soul destroying. After five years of remission, after daring to believe we might have a future free from cancer's shadow, it had returned. The weight of it was raw disbelief, overwhelming sadness and despair. We had been so close to freedom, but suddenly, it felt like we were back to square one. All the fear, uncertainty, and pain that we thought we had left behind came rushing back in.

We knew we were in for another battle, but this time it felt different, harder, more bitter. We had two young children now, and Richard had been through so much already. The thought of going through it all again was terrifying.

But we knew one thing for sure: we weren't giving up. We had made it through once, and we would fight again.

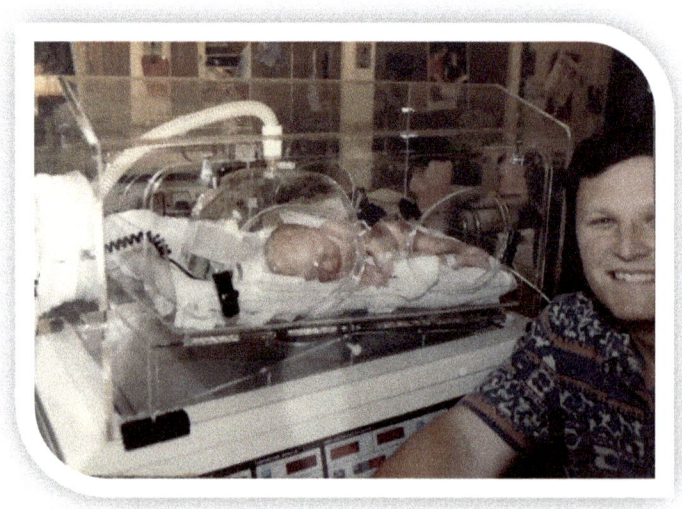

Richard with Emily

Chapter Four

Ebbs and Flows

It was 1997, and our lives had taken on a new rhythm, one that felt almost like the beginning of a fresh chapter. Emily was three and Nicholas was two. Our little family was full of energy and joy. We had just made a big move, about an hour north of Sydney, to the Central Coast. We bought a block of land and Richard, in what could only be described as a labour of love, poured his heart into orchestrating the build of our dream home. A beautiful split-level house with a pool, it was going to be our sanctuary.

Richard had always been a hands-on kind of guy. He relished the challenge of managing the build, and I could see how proud he was of what he was creating for us. Meanwhile, I had started a new job as a surgical Registered Nurse at a large Central Coast Hospital. It was a fresh start, and I threw myself into the work. Richard was still commuting to Sydney for his police job, but thankfully, the Police Force had transitioned to 12-hour shifts, which meant he only had to make the journey three days a week. The extra hours home with the kids and me were a blessing.

Life was full of the normal, chaotic juggle of family and work. We were busy, but happy, and enjoying the organised chaos that was our little family's life. But, always in the background, was the cancer. Richard's remission, the fragile peace we had known for five years, had ended. The shadow of Non-Hodgkins Lymphoma had returned.

With heavy hearts and a growing sense of dread, Richard and I went back to his hematology specialist and radiology oncologist. We knew what was coming. Chemotherapy. Radiotherapy. The cycle of hope and despair, the physical and emotional toll, all came rushing back. Richard was scheduled for another 12 weeks of treatment. It was like reliving a nightmare.

All the soul-destroying emotions came flooding back. The nausea, the fatigue, the uncertainty. I could hardly believe we were going through it all again. At that point, we had no idea that this was only the beginning. The next 15 years would be filled with treatments; chemotherapy, radiotherapy, trial after trial treatments, followed by endless six-monthly CT scans. Richard's doctors managed to keep the cancer at bay, treating it as it as it grew in size, but the hope of a 'cure' had been ripped from our reality and our desperately held tight grasp.

Even so, we tried to hold onto some sense of normality. We had two small children who needed us, who brought so much light and joy into our lives. They kept us grounded, reminding us of what we were fighting for. But the sheer weight of living with cancer, of never knowing if each round of treatment would be the last, or if there would always be another, loomed over everything.

Then, in 2001, just when we thought we had somewhat of a handle of living life with cancer and everything else, life threw us another surprise. I found out I was pregnant again.

It was a shock. If we hadn't thought it was possible to have Emily and Nicholas, we definitely didn't think it would happen again now, after everything Richard had been through. I remember staring at that pregnancy test, feeling a strange mix of disbelief, shock and hope. How was this even possible?

I wasn't sure whether to feel overjoyed or terrified. Richard had been through so much; his body had been pushed to its limits by the cancer and the treatments. We didn't know what this new pregnancy would mean for us, but there was one thing we knew for sure. We were being blessed with another chance to grow our family. And despite everything, we embraced it.

In 2001, not long after we'd discovered I was pregnant, Richard's cancer came back with a vengeance. It had spread to other lymph nodes in his abdomen, and we found ourselves thrust into the endless cycle of treatments once again. The doctors started new rounds of chemotherapy and radiotherapy, and we, as always, clung to hope, but it felt like a relentless battle with no end in sight.

At this point, Richard had transferred to a police station on the Central Coast, closer to home, which was great in many ways. He made good friends there, just as he had everywhere he worked. Richard had a knack for connecting with people. But then came the night that changed everything for Richard forever.

It's a night that's burned into my memory. Richard had been called out to a job, a traumatic incident that would haunt him for the rest of his life. He came home, pale and shaken, the weight of years on the frontline finally catching up with him. He told me about what had happened, but I could see something had shifted in him. He wasn't the same. That night, he made the decision to leave the Police Force on stress leave after 17 years of service. His mind and body had been pushed to their limits, and with the ongoing cancer treatments, it became too much to bear.

Emily was eight, Nicholas was six, and I was heavily pregnant. We were facing Richard's cancer head-on, and now the psychological trauma from his years in the police force was pulling him under as well. It felt like life was closing in on all sides.

But then, in what felt like divine timing, Zachary Jordan Bodle was born on the 5th of April, 2002, at 38 weeks. He was a healthy 8lbs 3oz and arrived by caesarean section. His birth brought us joy and relief, and in ways I couldn't have predicted, it was Zachary's arrival that saved Richard's life in ways that most of our family and friends were completely shielded and protected from. In the midst of his trauma and ongoing cancer battle, having a newborn baby boy to love and care for gave Richard's heart and soul a precious gift.

I returned to work full-time on night shifts when Zach was just five months old. It was hard leaving my little family, but Richard, who wasn't working at the time due to his treatments and trauma recovery, became Zach's full-time parent. And he thrived in the role. Those first couple of years, Richard was front and centre for Emily, Nicholas and Zach. They all formed a deep bond, and Richard was a hands-on dad in every way. Sure, there were a few moments where he may have 'temporarily misplaced' Zach, but overall, he was a top-shelf, first-class dad.

Not only was Richard an amazing dad with Zach, but he also threw himself into the kids' activities. He'd take Emily to her netball games and training, always the over-enthusiastic parent on the sideline, cheering her on. Emily loved having him there, even if his enthusiasm was a bit much at times! And he was just as dedicated to Nicholas, taking him to soccer and later rugby union, proudly watching him from the sidelines, and again being vocally enthusiastic.

Richard even became our family's regular chef. He enjoyed being in the kitchen, experimenting with new recipes and flavours. He had toyed with the idea of becoming a chef as his Grandfather had been in Canada. He talked about it sometimes, wondering if it might be a new direction for him. Despite all the challenges and battles he was facing. Cancer. The trauma from his police work; Richard never stopped being present for our family. He was an incredible dad and partner, and I could see how much joy he took in our children's lives.

Richard's health may have been a rollercoaster, but through it all, he never stopped giving his best to us. His strength, even in the face of so much adversity, was something that carried us all through. And little Zach, in his own way, was just a blessing.

One thing Richard and I didn't always agree on was how to handle telling the kids about his cancer. Richard, ever the protector, didn't want to worry them. He wanted to protect Emily and Nicholas from the heavy burden of knowing that their dad was fighting such a serious illness. I completely understood his feelings, but I had a different perspective. I wanted them to know, particularly when Richard was in good health. I felt strongly that they should understand that cancer didn't automatically mean terrible sickness or death, and that people can live with it, even thrive for long periods of time.

I had always feared them hearing it from someone else, which, unfortunately, is exactly what happened. Emily was about 12 years old when she overheard someone mention Richard's cancer, and it broke my heart. It wasn't how we wanted her to find out, and I could see the confusion and fear in her eyes when she came to us, full of questions we weren't ready to answer just yet. That moment solidified what I had been feeling for a long time. We needed to be open with the kids.

So, Richard and I sat down together and decided it was time to tell both Emily and Nicholas. Thankfully, Richard was in a good place health-wise at the time, looking strong and feeling well. We gathered them together one afternoon, and with as much care, love and honesty and age-appropriate information as possible, explained that their dad had cancer. Of course, the first question out of their mouths was the one we dreaded most: "Is Dad going to die?"

It's the question no parent ever wants to hear from their child, but we were ready. We explained it to them in a way they could understand, sharing the truth without overwhelming them. We told them that while cancer is a serious illness, Dad was fighting it with all the help that modern medicine could provide, and that many people live with it for years. We wanted them to know that, yes, it was tough, but their dad was strong, and we had every reason to hope for many more good days and years ahead.

What amazed me most was how children are so much more resilient than we give them credit for. Emily and Nicholas took everything we said in their stride. They asked their questions, listened carefully, and then, just like that, they seemed to move on. There were no dramatic changes in behaviour or fear-filled days; they just kept living their little lives, full with school, friends, and sports. It was almost as if telling them lightened a load we didn't even realise we were carrying.

In a way, their response made our lives easier. We no longer had to tiptoe around the topic, worried about what they might overhear or wonder. It was out in the open, and we could talk about it honestly when we needed to. That openness brought a sense of relief, not just for me, but I think for Richard too, even if he was reluctant to admit it. The kids knew, and life went on, even with cancer as part of the picture now.

We cherished family holidays, especially the ones when Richard was feeling well and wasn't in the midst of treatment. One holiday that stands out was our trip to Fiji. Emily was ten, Nicholas was eight, and little Zach was just 18 months old. It was our first overseas trip as a family, and we were all buzzing with excitement.

Of course, for the trip to happen, the kids needed passports. Richard, being the go-getter he was, took on the task of sorting out all the legal documentation. I remember waking up after a night shift to find Richard proudly presenting me with a stack of completed passport paperwork. He had filled out everything, and I could tell he was expecting me to be impressed.

Well, I was, just not in the way he had hoped. As I skimmed through the forms, I quickly realised that I was impressed that he had got all their middle names and birth dates wrong. It was a classic Richard moment: meticulous in his enthusiasm but a bit off in the details. The paperwork was a bit of a debacle, but it was filled with his love and good intentions!

We had a good laugh over it, and despite the paperwork mishaps, we got everything sorted in time. The trip itself was magical. We swam and snorkeled in the crystal-clear waters, lounged on sun-drenched beaches, and enjoyed the vibrant Fijian culture. Emily, Nicholas, and Zach loved every moment, and seeing their joy and wonder made the holiday even more special.

Richard's ability to keep things light-hearted, even when he wasn't feeling his best, was one of the many things I loved about him. The holiday was a much-needed escape and a reminder of how precious family time was. It wasn't just about the destinations or the activities, but the simple joy of being together, creating memories that would carry us through the tougher times.

We often look back on those holidays with fondness, knowing that despite the struggles we faced, we made the most of our time together. Richard's unwavering spirit and love for his family made every adventure, no matter how small, unforgettable.

Enjoying life

Chapter Five

Chain of Events

In January 2012, we received news that we always dreaded but was constantly at the back of our minds. Richard's 6 monthly scan showed that his lymphoma was progressing yet again, despite all the endless rounds of treatments, trials, and experimental drugs he had already endured. It was as though we were in an endless cycle, and every time we thought we were a step ahead, the cancer found a way to claw its way back.

At this point, Richard's hematologist decided it was time to go down the bone marrow transplant route. It had always been a viable option to use sometime in the future if needed, but we had hoped we might never need to go there. Now, it was no longer a distant possibility, it was the next step. But before we could even think about the transplant, Richard needed to go through yet another round of aggressive chemotherapy to push the cancer back into remission. Without that, the transplant couldn't happen.

The first step in the transplant process was to find a bone marrow match. Naturally, Richard's three sisters were the first to be tested. We had all been hopeful, thinking that at least one of them would be a match, particularly his twin sister. But, heartbreakingly, none of them were a match for Richard, even though they all matched each other. It was just one of those cruel ironies we seemed to encounter so often on this cancer journey.

With no familial match, his medical team turned to the worldwide bone marrow register, a database of potential donors across the globe. This was a huge waiting game, and the anticipation was almost unbearable. We knew the odds weren't necessarily in our favour, but we were holding on to whatever hope we could.

Then, the news came. There was one match. One single match out of the entire worldwide register. A lady in Germany. She was a perfect 10/10 match. I remember the moment they told us; it felt surreal, like something out of a movie. Could it really be true? Could this stranger on the other side of the world be the one to give Richard the gift of life?

When she was notified, she agreed without hesitation to proceed with the donation. The selflessness of this stranger was overwhelming. It was an unbelievable gift, something that felt almost too good to be true. I remember us sitting in disbelief, our emotions torn between cautious optimism and the sinking feeling that somehow, there might be another twist.

This was our glimmer of hope, though, and we clung to it fiercely. Richard, ever the pragmatist, focused on the immediate challenge, getting through the chemotherapy to ensure the transplant could even take place. And while I tried to stay hopeful, there was always that nagging fear in the back of my mind. Would this finally be the answer we had been waiting for, or was it just another chapter in an already long, difficult and heartbreaking at times story?

The road ahead was daunting, but knowing there was someone out there willing to help a complete stranger gave us a sense of renewed strength. It reminded us that even in the darkest moments, there's kindness in the world, and sometimes that's enough to keep you going.

The wheels were set in motion, and Richard was ready to undergo the bone marrow transplant as soon as he had reached remission. It felt like we had a plan in place. It was a final step that could potentially save his life. In early 2012, he began another grueling round of chemotherapy, this time with the singular goal of getting him into remission for the transplant.

For six long weeks, we endured the rollercoaster that chemo had become. Endless hospital visits, the unbearable side effects, and the constant ticking of time. But we as always, feared and hoped at the same time that at the end of it all, we'd get the news we were so desperate to hear: that the chemo was working, that the cancer was retreating.

Then came the devastating blow. Instead of shrinking, Richard's cancer had actually grown. It was that shattering blow we had become all too used to. After everything we'd been through, all the treatments, the endless battles, and now this, our best shot, had seemingly failed. I remember the crushing sense of disbelief washing over us. It wasn't just disappointment; it was like the world had turned upside down. What now? Where did we go from here? Was there even a next step?

We felt utterly hopeless for a time. There was nothing to hold on to. It's like you've spent years fighting this unseen enemy, and just when you think you're about to win, the enemy comes back stronger, mocking you for your efforts.

But Richard's medical team wasn't ready to give up, and neither were we. His hematologists managed to get him onto a new chemotherapy trial that had originated in Germany. This was the only other option left at the time. It was a long shot. Richard had a one-in-three chance of being selected for the trial. We barely dared to hope. After so much disappointment, we were bracing ourselves for more bad news.

And yet, Richard got in.

It felt like a miracle. That one-in-three chance had come through. It was hard not to feel hopeful again, but we tempered it with caution, knowing how quickly things could change.

The new German chemotherapy was, for us, surprisingly effective. And after his first round, the results were remarkable. His next scan showed that his cancer had finally started to shrink. We were stunned. Relieved. Overwhelmed. After months of spiralling downward, we were finally moving in the right direction. It was like the sun had broken through the clouds after a long, dark storm.

For the first time in a long time, we allowed ourselves to feel real hope. Maybe, just maybe, this was going to be the breakthrough we needed. The possibility of the bone marrow transplant was back on the table, and with each scan showing further progress, we started to believe that remission and that life-saving transplant was within reach again.

Up until this time, 2012 had been a rollercoaster ride, filled with highs and lows, but at that moment, it felt like we were finally moving forward. We clung to that glimmer of hope, focusing on the bone marrow transplant that was now, once again, within reach. Richard had completed the trial chemotherapy by spring, and although it had been a gruelling stretch, it had worked. His cancer was in remission, and we were back on track for the transplant, now scheduled for November 2012.

It was surreal to think about how close we were to this critical moment. The transplant team explained the process in detail, how they would fly to Germany to collect the bone marrow from this amazing lady who had agreed to be Richard's donor. They would retrieve the marrow and bring it back immediately, without freezing it, to ensure it was as fresh as possible for the transplant. It was all carefully planned, almost a military-like operation, and we were in awe of the effort and coordination involved.

Before the big day, Richard's transplant team suggested something unexpected. They encouraged us to take a short family holiday. They believed that both Richard and our family needed some time to rest, regroup, and mentally recharge after everything we had been through over the past year. Richard's body, too, needed time to regain strength after months of chemotherapy.

It felt a bit strange at first, the idea of going on a holiday while such a huge procedure loomed over us. But the more we thought about it, the more we realised how important this break would be. The bone marrow transplant wasn't going to be easy. The recovery period was projected to take anywhere from 6 to 12 months. It was going to be another tough road ahead, and we all needed to prepare for that, both physically and mentally.

So, we planned a simple getaway. Nothing extravagant, just a quiet family escape where we could unwind, spend time together, and let our bodies and minds rest. The kids were excited, and for a brief moment, it felt like we could put the weight of cancer to the side, even if just for a little while.

That holiday ended up being exactly what we needed. It wasn't about ticking off tourist spots or grand adventures. It was about soaking in those moments of togetherness, spending our days on the beach together, swimming, surfing, theme parks and enjoying the warmer weather and sunshine. We weren't just regaining strength physically, but emotionally as well. It was a chance to remember that beyond the doctors, hospitals, and treatments, we were a family. And that was what we were fighting for.

October was supposed to be our chance to breathe, to put the stress of the year behind us for a bit and spend some quality family time together. We headed to Burleigh Heads in Queensland and booked a waterfront high-rise apartment for ten days. It was the perfect spot for a family escape. Emily was 18, Nicholas 17, and Zach 10. We'd left our one-year-old cocker spaniel, Bella Bublé Bodle, at a 5-star pet resort, feeling assured she would be well cared for while we were away. She was part of the family, and we trusted she'd be in good hands.

Everything was going smoothly until Monday morning, 3 days after we had left. I got a phone call from the pet resort, and straight away, I knew something was wrong. The person on the other end told me they'd found Bella completely paralysed, except for her eye movement. They suspected a paralysis tick, which is a common but deadly danger for pets in Australia. My heart sank.

It was a long weekend, and the resort had rushed her to an after-hours emergency vet. Despite the vet's best efforts and the reversal tick treatment they administered, Bella wasn't responding. They explained that if there was any chance at all, she would need to be transferred to Sydney and put on life support, as there were no machines left available on the Central Coast. And even then, there was no guarantee she'd survive. The vet had been honest with us. It was a slim hope, and Bella was already in a critical state.

I remember feeling completely helpless, caught between wanting to be there with Bella and knowing that this holiday was meant to be a time for us to recharge, especially for Richard before his transplant. The kids were devastated. Emily was crying, pleading to go home and be with her, but we had to weigh everything up. The year had been so heavy already, and this was supposed to be our break, our regrouping moment as a family after months of chaos and worry.

Richard and I had some difficult conversations over the next couple of days, as we tried to balance emotions, logistics, and Bella's suffering. After 48 hours of heartbreak, and having already spent $4,000 on emergency care due to the public holiday, we had to make an incredibly hard and sad decision, we chose to stop all treatment for Bella and let her go peacefully by herself while we stayed in Queensland.

It felt unfair, like another cruel twist of fate. This was supposed to be a time for healing and happiness, and yet we found ourselves saying goodbye to a beloved family member. I felt guilty, crushed, and powerless all at once. The kids, as were we, absolutely guttered, but they understood. Bella was part of the family, and losing her in such an unexpected way made our holiday incredibly bittersweet.

A beautiful friend I worked with at the Hospital went to the vets for us to say goodbye and take some photos, to help us say goodbye and grieve our little Bella Bublé Bodle.

As much as the kids and I wanted to go back home for Bella, I had to look at the bigger picture and remember why we were all away at this time. Maybe it was the wrong decision, maybe it was the right one, but we stayed, and I was beyond determined to make this holiday what it was intended to be.

In the midst of it all, we tried to salvage what we could of the holiday. Richard, Emily, and Nicholas surfed. We hung out at the beach most days and went to White Water World and Dreamworld. We actually ended up having a great family holiday with fun and loving memories.

We were there to regroup, to find some calm before Richard's next big hurdle with his bone marrow transplant, and even though we were all carrying the weight of Bella's loss, we still had moments of laughter, connection, and a sense of togetherness that we so badly needed. Those 10 days in Burleigh Heads became a symbol of resilience in many ways. It wasn't the relaxing, carefree holiday we had imagined, but it was a reminder of how we continued to hold each other up, even in the hardest of times. That little holiday felt like a deep breath before the plunge. When we returned home, we were ready to face the next chapter, the transplant, and everything that came with it.

We didn't know it at the time, but that was to be our last ever family holiday together.

 When we got home, the house felt emptier without Bella, but we knew we'd done the right thing. It was just another challenge in a long string of them, but we faced it like we did everything else, with love and support for one another.

Our minds shifted quickly to the intense preparation required for Richard's upcoming bone marrow transplant. We were fully aware of how crucial this next step was in his fight. The plan was for Richard to be admitted to the hospital a week before the transplant for daily chemotherapy and the day before the transplant full-body radiation. This would essentially wipe out his immune system, a necessary step to ensure his body wouldn't reject the new bone marrow. Along with the anti-rejection drugs he would then need to take post transplant, it felt like all the pieces were finally coming together for this chance at life.

The date was set. Richard was scheduled to go into the hospital in November, and we had been mentally preparing for the challenges ahead. But a phone call 2 weeks out from the transplant literally changed everything, and in that moment, the world again came crashing down around us again. The bone marrow donor from Germany, our one perfect match in the entire world, had pulled out at the eleventh hour.

We weren't given any explanation, and due to the Privacy Act, we weren't entitled to one. There was no closure, no understanding, just a blunt and devastating reality. I still remember that sinking feeling in my chest, a mixture of shock and anger. We had placed so much hope in this transplant. This was supposed to be Richard's chance at a possible cure from his cancer and to finally turn the corner. Now it was gone. Just like that.

It was soul-destroying. I felt betrayed by a faceless system, as though everything we had fought so hard for had been ripped away just when we thought we were on the verge of something hopeful. How many times can one person be knocked down before it all becomes too much? How many times can you pick yourself up, only to be knocked down again? It felt endless, exhausting, and deeply unfair.

But Richard, as always, showed his remarkable resilience. He didn't crumble. He didn't let this setback define the rest of his battle. He faced the news with a quiet dignity, the same courage and strength that had carried him through the last 21 years. He had asked me, during one of his darkest moments, "Why me?" but that was the one and only time I ever heard him question his fate. He refused to be defined by the illness. He simply kept going, no matter how many times life tried to break him.

So, we found ourselves once again in a state of uncertainty. The looming question hung over us: now what? Where do we go from here? Was there even time to find another suitable donor? Could we go through this process again, the endless waiting, the hope, the potential disappointment? It was overwhelming to think about.

The transplant team immediately went back to the worldwide donor register. The urgency was palpable. Time was of the essence, and we didn't know how much of it we had left as we didn't know how long he would be able to stay in remission for. Every day counted, but the clock kept ticking, and we were back in limbo, stuck in this agonising waiting game.

But through all of this, Richard stayed focused. He didn't let the despair swallow him, even though I knew deep down he must have been feeling all of it. He just kept moving forward, even when the path ahead was unclear. It was his unwavering faith and strength that kept all of us going. He fought with everything he had, and so did we.

That period was one of the most challenging of our lives. We didn't know what the future held, but what I did know was that no matter what came next, Richard was never alone in this fight. We had faced so much together already, and we would continue to face whatever came next, side by side, no matter how hard it got.

We didn't realise it at the time, but Richard's remission was like a ticking time bomb. The window for the transplant was shrinking, and every day counted while he remained in remission. There was no way to know how long the trial chemotherapy would keep his cancer at bay, and we were constantly on edge. The pressure was mounting to find a suitable donor before the remission slipped away, and with it, the chance for a life-saving bone marrow transplant.

Two potential donors had been identified on the worldwide register; one in America with a 9/10 match and another in Germany again with an 8/10 match. Neither obviously a perfect 10/10, but they were still possibilities. However, the bone marrow team and Richard's hematologists wanted to explore all avenues, including testing Emily and Nicholas as potential donors. Being his children, there was a chance they could be a perfect match, even though the odds weren't high, at the very least a 5/10 match.

I remember the day vividly. I took Emily and Nicholas to the hospital for their blood tests. It was a sombre moment, filled with hope and trepidation. While the kids sat waiting, a nurse discreetly pulled me aside. She gently explained that, because the genetic makeup would be clearly visible in the results, now was the time to confidentially disclose if there was any chance Richard might not be their biological father. I was shocked for a second but quickly reassured her that there was no need for concern. Richard was their father, in every way possible, and this was just another step in our journey together as a family.

Emily and Nicholas had their blood tests done, and then we waited. The results came back a few days later, confirming that they were both 5/10 matches, half of Richard's and my combined genetic makeup. It was a mixed result; not perfect, but not out of the question either.

After much consultation, collaboration, and deliberation between the transplant team, hematologists, and experts, they decided that Nicholas, being a male and a direct blood relative, would be the best option. It was surreal to think that our 17-year-old son could be the one to give his father the fighting chance of life. Despite the weight of the situation, Nicholas never hesitated for a second. There was no fear or reluctance in him. He just wanted to help his dad, and he was fully committed to doing whatever it took.

As parents, we found ourselves navigating new territory, worrying not just for Richard's health but for Nicholas too. The pressure was immense, but in our hearts, we knew that we were doing everything we could, as a family, to give Richard the best possible chance.

Through it all, Richard maintained his quiet strength, and Nicholas displayed a level of bravery that I will never forget. This was a battle we were fighting together, and it reminded me once again of the resilience that had carried us through all these years.

Zach, Emily and Nicholas

Chapter Six

Harsh Realities

Nicholas, in his final year of high school, was about to begin his second term of Year 12. We knew this would have a significant impact on his studies, but Nicholas never wavered in his commitment to helping his dad. It was a lot for a young man to take on, but he carried himself with such quiet strength. We tried to balance the demands of his schooling with the gravity of what was ahead, knowing that this was a life-changing experience for all of us.

Two weeks before the transplant was scheduled, Nicholas began the necessary injections to stimulate the release of bone marrow from his bones into his bloodstream. I administered these injections to him twice a day. As the doctors had warned us, after a few days, Nicholas started to experience deep aches in his bones as the bone marrow was being drawn out. It was painful, and I could see the discomfort in his eyes, but he never complained. He just pushed through, determined to help his dad.

Meanwhile, Richard went into hospital one week before the transplant date, set for February 22, 2013, to begin his week of chemotherapy. This was an intense period. Richard needed to be as prepared as possible for the transplant. The chemotherapy was brutal, as it always was, but he was resolute. He had been through so much already, and this was just another hurdle in a long journey.

On the day he was admitted, the doctors also inserted a PICC (peripherally inserted central catheter) line into one of the large veins near his heart. This would give long-term access for all the treatments he would need, including chemotherapy, the bone marrow transplant itself, intravenous antibiotics, and a cocktail of other IV medications he would require throughout the process.

During this time, I found myself juggling multiple roles. I would drive to Sydney every day to be with Richard in the hospital, spending hours by his side to support him through the chemotherapy. Then, in the afternoons, I'd rush back home to the Central Coast to be there for Emily, Nicholas, and Zach when they returned from school and Uni. It was a whirlwind of emotions, physical exhaustion, and constant worry, but it was what needed to be done. We were all in this together, and it was my way of making sure we didn't lose sight of that.

Nicholas, even while dealing with the effects of the injections and the stress of school, continued attending his Year 12 classes. His teachers were aware of the situation, and the school was amazingly supportive, which was a relief and very reassuring. But still, it was a lot for a 17-year-old to handle. Emily and Zach were also incredibly supportive, though I knew it was hard for them to watch their dad go through this once again. They had grown up with the shadow of Richard's illness looming over them, and yet they never let it overwhelm them. Their resilience was remarkable.

The day before the transplant, Richard underwent full-body radiotherapy, total body irradiation, to further suppress his immune system. This was a critical step to ensure his body wouldn't reject the bone marrow transplant. It was an exhausting process, both physically, emotionally and mentally, but he faced it with his usual stoicism, knowing this was the final step before the transplant.

By now, we had been through so many ups and downs that we had learned to take things one day at a time. Each day was a small victory in itself. The fear of the unknown was ever-present, but we held onto hope. This was our chance to hopefully finally rid Richard's body of the cancer that had plagued him for so long, and we were ready to face whatever came next.

February 22nd was approaching fast, and we were as prepared as we could be, both physically and emotionally. The transplant was just around the corner, and though we didn't know what the future held, we knew we and Richards team of Drs had done everything in their power to get to this point. Nicholas was about to make an extraordinary sacrifice for his dad, and the weight of that was not lost on any of us. We could only hope that this would be the breakthrough we had been waiting for.

Despite the gruelling week Richard had endured, he was holding up remarkably well, considering the intensity of the chemotherapy and the full-body radiation. He was tired, naturally, but his spirit remained unbroken. The journey we had been on to reach this day had been long and filled with countless setbacks, but here we were, finally at the day we had been waiting for: transplant day.

On the morning of February 22nd, I brought Nicholas to the hospital at 8am as instructed. He had been so brave leading up to this moment, never once showing hesitation or fear about the procedure, even though I knew it wasn't going to be easy. The medical team quickly got him set up, and soon enough, Nicholas was hooked up to the machine that would draw out his bone marrow from his blood stream.

The process was explained to us beforehand in simple terms, but witnessing it was something else. They inserted a large needle into Nicholas's left arm to extract his blood, which would then pass through a machine designed to filter out the precious bone marrow. The rest of his blood was returned to his body through another large needle in his right arm. The setup looked daunting, and I could see the slight tension in Nicholas's face as the process began, but he never complained. This procedure would take about six hours, and Nicholas would have to remain still the entire time. It was a long, slow process, but one filled with so much hope.

For a short while, Richard was able to leave his hospital room and come sit with Nicholas during that 6hr process. Seeing them together during such a monumental moment, father and son, one literally giving part of himself to save the other, changed me forever. Richard, despite his own physical exhaustion, pulled a chair up beside Nicholas's bed, offering him a quiet kind support. They didn't need to say much. The weight of the moment spoke for itself.

As the hours ticked by, I could see Nicholas growing more tired. The process of siphoning bone marrow was taxing, both physically and mentally. But he stayed strong, knowing that what he was doing could potentially save his dad's life. I stayed nearby, feeling that familiar mix of pride and anxiety. There were moments where the gravity of it all hit me like a wave, but I knew I had to stay composed for both of them. This was our reality; waiting, hoping, praying for the best.

Finally, after six long hours, the machine finished its work. Nicholas was pale and understandably tired, but he had done it. The medical team carefully collected the precious bone marrow that had been filtered from Nicholas's blood, and it was immediately prepped for Richard's transplant. I remember them remarking how healthy the colour of his bone marrow looked. Nicholas was given some time to rest and recover after the procedure, while the transplant team prepared Richard for what would come next.

This was it. It was the culmination of months of preparation, treatments, setbacks, and hope. The bone marrow Nicholas had so selflessly donated was now ready to be transplanted into Richard. It was such a surreal moment, knowing that part of our son was about to be infused into Richard, giving him the best possible chance of a possible cancer cure, or at least the gift of more time with us all, however long that may be. The transplant itself was almost anticlimactic in its simplicity.

That afternoon, Richard lay quietly in his hospital room as the life-saving bone marrow from our son Nicholas flowed into his body through the PICC line. The whole process, while profound in its significance, was almost unremarkable. In just under an hour and a half, the transfusion was complete. I sat by his side the entire time, quietly watching the steady drip, feeling a mixture of relief, hope and cautious optimism. This was the moment we'd been waiting for.

My sister Victoria had taken Nicholas home to rest after his long and exhausting day. He was still sore from the procedure, but his spirits were high knowing what he had done for his dad. Meanwhile, I stayed with Richard, grateful that the transplant had gone smoothly, without any immediate complications. It felt like a huge weight had been lifted from our shoulders. For the first time in what felt like forever, we allowed ourselves to feel hopeful, happy, and even a little excited about the future.

But the journey wasn't over yet. Because Nicholas was a related donor, there was an increased risk of Richard's body rejecting the bone marrow. To minimize this, Richard was given another two days of double-strength chemotherapy. It was of course incredibly hard on him and incredibly hard to watch. His body already weakened from the previous rounds of treatment and the transplant itself. This extra step was necessary, but it took a toll on him.

Soon after this chemotherapy Richard began to feel unwell. The doctors reassured us that it was 'normal transplant and double chemotherapy unwell', a vague but strangely comforting phrase. It was expected for him to develop a fever, and sure enough, his temperature spiked.

He became nauseated and started vomiting, his blood pressure plummeted, and his heart rate soared. I watched helplessly as he was hooked up to more monitors and IV lines. His once strong body was now frail and vulnerable, enduring yet another round of physical hardship.

Blood cultures were taken immediately to rule out any infections, and Richard was moved from his single room in the transplant unit to a negative pressured single room. This was a precautionary measure until the test results came back, and although it was unsettling, the medical team assured me it was standard protocol. The room itself felt isolating, with heavy doors and a sterile, air-locked environment to prevent the spread or further exposure of any possible infections.

I remember sitting there all gowned up with gloves and a mask on watching him sleep on and off, wires and tubes connected to his body, and wondering how much more he could take. The transplant had been a success in terms of the procedure, but the aftermath was brutal. Every moment was a reminder of how fragile this situation was. The hope we had felt just days earlier now had to be tempered with the harsh reality of recovery.

The days that followed were some of the hardest. Richard's body was weak, and he faced more side effects from the double chemotherapy. But through it all, he remained resilient, as did we. We had come too far to lose hope now. All we could do was wait for his body to recover, wait for the new bone marrow to take and begin its work, and wait for the day when we could finally start thinking about life beyond this hospital room.

In those quiet hours, as Richard drifted in and out of sleep, I kept reminding myself that this was part of the process. That things were going according to plan, no matter how terrifying it felt and looked in the moment. The transplant team was incredibly attentive, checking his vitals, his wellbeing, adjusting his medications, and monitoring every aspect of his recovery. Their confidence in the process helped ease some of the anxiety, but as a wife and mother, there was still that ever present worry lingering in the background.

At the same time, life outside the hospital continued. Emily, Nicholas, and Zach were all doing their best to maintain a sense of normalcy while their dad fought through this. Emily, now 19 and mature beyond her years, had stepped up in so many ways, helping with her brothers and keeping things running smoothly at home while studying. Nicholas, despite the physical strain of donating his bone marrow, was back at school, trying to focus on his Year 12 studies. Zach, still just a little boy, coped in his own way, busy at school and holding onto the hope that his dad would come home soon.

Zach unfortunately couldn't see his dad after the transplant as he wasn't allowed in the transplant unit. Children under 12 years were deemed to carry too many potential germs and bugs on their person to enter the unit, and so we of course complied.

Richard still had one more round of double-strength chemotherapy to endure. Watching him go through it was gut wrenching. His once strong and capable body was now so weak, and the side effects of the treatment were taking their toll. He had little energy left, and his appetite had completely disappeared. Most days, he barely touched his food, I tried to encourage him to eat and brought in his favourite foods. He slept for long stretches, exhausted by the battle his body was fighting, and I often found myself just sitting quietly by his side feeling incredibly helpless but ever hopeful.

Thankfully, after what felt like an eternity of waiting, the blood culture results came back as negative. It was a huge relief knowing that no infections had taken root amidst everything else he was dealing with. The doctors were able to move him out of the negative pressure room and back into a single room in the transplant unit, which felt like a small step forward.

But the real test, whether the bone marrow transplant had started to take and work, was still ahead of us. The doctors had warned us that it may take around 10 to 14 days before we'd see any signs in his blood tests that the transplant had 'taken.' By the one week mark, there was still no indication that the new bone marrow had begun to graft and take effect. This was expected, but it didn't stop the nagging worry that sat heavy in my chest every day.

As the days passed, Richard's condition continued to deteriorate. He was becoming increasingly unwell, and it was hard not to feel the weight of dread creeping in. From day eight to day twelve, I could see that he was struggling more and more. His team of doctors were monitoring him closely, and he was getting every form of support available, IV fluids, IV antibiotics, IV electrolytes and pain management, but still, his body wasn't responding the way we had hoped.

By day twelve, there was still no sign in his blood work that the transplant had taken. The doctors had explained that this was not unusual and that we still had time, but watching him decline before my eyes was terrifying. Every day felt like a lifetime, waiting for that crucial piece of news that would tell us the bone marrow was doing its job. It was hard to stay positive when each day seemed to bring more complications and setbacks.

Richard however, as always, remained quietly resilient. Even in his weakened state, he never really complained. There were no dramatic moments of despair from him, just a quiet endurance. He had been through so much already;

years of treatments, setbacks, and this never ending fight against cancer, and somehow, he still carried on. But I could see in his eyes, even when they were half-closed from fatigue, that he was exhausted, not just physically but emotionally and mentally.

I tried my best to be strong for him, for the kids, for myself. But it was getting harder each day to stay optimistic, as the reality of the situation weighed heavily on us all. We were in the most critical period, and there was little we could do but wait and hope that his body would start to accept Nicholas's bone marrow and begin to heal.

We had already gone through so much as a family, and I couldn't help but wonder how much more Richard's body could take. We were holding on to the doctors words, 10 to 14 days, but with every passing day, the anxiety deepened. The transplant team remained cautiously optimistic, reminding us that the process could be slow, especially given everything Richard had been through in the months leading up to the transplant.

Still, it was impossible to ignore the fact that he was getting worse, not better. His energy was fading, his weight had dropped significantly, and he spent most of the time either asleep or in a fog of exhaustion. Each time a nurse or doctor came into the room to check on him, his vitals or adjust his medications, I found myself holding my breath, waiting for any small sign that things were starting to turn around.

The kids were struggling with their own emotions. Nicholas, after giving so much of himself to help his dad, was trying to balance the stress of everything at home with his final year of school. Emily was quietly anxious, doing her best to be supportive, while Zach, still so young, didn't fully understand the gravity of the situation but knew something wasn't right.

As we reached day twelve without any positive signs, it felt like we were standing on the edge of a cliff, unsure of what was to come. We knew the next few days would be crucial, and all we could do was wait.

I continued my daily routine of going to Sydney in the mornings to be with Richard, then heading home in the afternoons to be with the kids. It was a delicate balancing act, trying to be there for him while also being present for Emily, Nicholas, and Zach. On Tuesday afternoon, day twelve post-transplant, I had spent the morning and early afternoon with Richard as I had every day.

He was so weak, sick, lost in a delirium that was hard and sad to witness, and I was terrified. I could see the flicker of fear in his eyes, a stark contrast to the resilient spirit he'd always shown. That day, he begged me, almost desperately, to somehow go back in time and not go ahead with the transplant. His words broke my heart and my soul. I had hoped this would be the turning point for us, a step towards healing. I held his hand and hoped he found comfort in my presence, but I could see that he was losing hope.

I helped him walk to the bathroom with his drip that afternoon. Every step was a monumental effort for him, and I felt a wave of sadness wash over me as I realized how far he had fallen since the day of the transplant. Once he was back in bed, I held his hand and prayed while he fell asleep, hoping he could find some peace in those fleeting moments of rest. As I watched him drift off, I couldn't shake the feeling that something was terribly wrong, but I brushed it aside, determined to remain hopeful.

I went home to the kids once he was asleep, my heart heavy with deep concern but trying to focus on their world too. Emily and Nicholas were busy with their studies, and Zach was playing with his toys and games, blissfully unaware of the gravity of the situation. I cooked dinner, forced smiles, and made light conversation, all while an overwhelming worry and fear hovered at me like a persistent shadow.

That would be the last time I would ever see Richard conscious again.

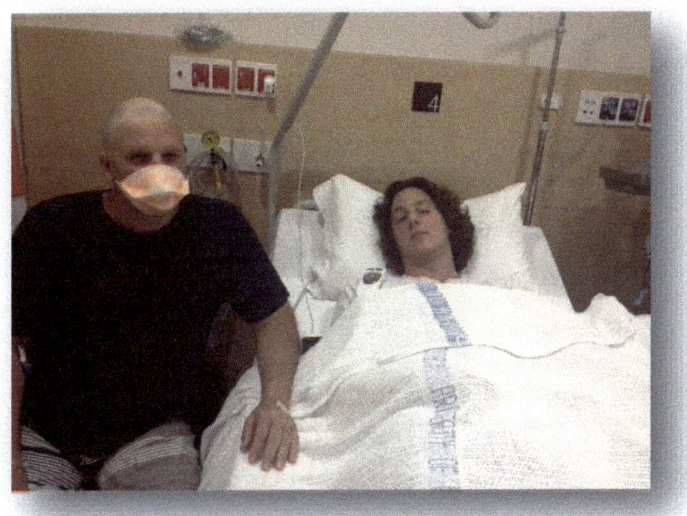

Richard and Nicholas

Chapter Seven

The Funeral

The day after Richard died, a representative from our church came to our house to begin funeral arrangements. I felt like I was again trapped in a nightmare that I couldn't wake up from. The world outside continued on, oblivious to the devastation I was experiencing. I was in complete and utter disbelief and distress as to what had happened less than 24 hours before. I didn't know which way was up and certainly didn't have any capacity to make any decisions or face making funeral arrangements for my husband and the father of our children.

Thank goodness for my sister Victoria. She was on long service leave at this time and had come to stay with me. Her presence was a lifeline, grounding me amid the chaos. She took charge when I felt completely lost, helping me navigate the practicalities while I was submerged in my grief. I remember feeling like I was in a frightening and terrifying fog, totally incapable of making decisions or choices. My mind was heavy, weighed down by sorrow. All I could do was cry and cry and cry, each sob tearing at the fabric of my heart and soul.

As the funeral representative spoke, I barely registered the words. It was as if I was hearing them through a tunnel, distant and muffled. The only thing that broke through my haze was when they suggested that the words at the top of the Order of Service say: 'Celebrating the Life of Richard Bodle.' My gut reaction was visceral. There was no way I was having that written on there! I was sad. I was angry. Why would we be celebrating what had just happened?!

In that moment of raw emotion, I felt a flicker of clarity amid the storm. I shook my head, fighting back more tears. I choose the familiar but far less 'offensive' option: 'In Loving Memory of Richard Bodle.' It felt right. It felt real. It was a reflection of the ache in my heart, the loss that loomed so large. I remember the representative looking at me, perhaps surprised, but I could see understanding in his eyes. If, at that point in time, I had to speak up, speak from my heart, and make a decision, it was this one.

And I have never regretted it.

The days that followed were a blur. Victoria helped me through taking care of so many details that needed attention — meeting with the funeral home with and all the decisions that came with that, joined by Richard's mum and sisters Diane and Sarah, and coordinating with the church with the upcoming Service. I sat at home overwhelmed with absolutely everything, staring into space, my thoughts a jumbled mess. Our children of course were also in shock, navigating their own grief in their own ways. Emily and Nicholas's friends were amazing, coming to our home to support them and take them out at times, and Zach, only ten, was too young to fully grasp the permanence of what had happened but couldn't be shielded from the raw sadness that engulfed us. He literally spent one day at home after Richard died then begged me to go back to school to be with his friends and, looking back, he just needed some concrete 'normality' in his life that had changed forever.

I felt like I was on autopilot, doing what needed to be done, but I was craving 'normality' too, and not really present for any of it. At times, I would catch myself thinking of Richard—his laughter, his smile, the way he would tease me about the tiniest things. And then the crushing weight of reality would hit me all over again. It was unbearable.

As the week went on, seemingly hurtling towards a funeral I couldn't believe was going to happen, I had decided at this point that neither I nor our children would be going. Richard wasn't meant to die. This wasn't the future his bone marrow transplant could have and should have been! My heart screamed for the life we were supposed to have together, for the laughter and joy that was so cruelly taken from us. I couldn't and wouldn't subject our children and myself to any more emotional trauma than we had already been through. I honestly thought that by not attending the funeral, I could somehow shield us from the pain, from the overwhelming finality of it all.

But then again, I was in such a fog of grief that rational thinking was a foreign concept in my world at that time. I couldn't see the whole picture, the importance of saying goodbye, of having a chance to honour Richard and what he meant to us. I was focused on survival, on keeping the kids safe from any more heartache, and I convinced myself that avoiding the funeral was the best way to do that.

Thankfully, Victoria saw right through my reasoning. One evening, as I sat on the couch, utterly exhausted from the weight of everything, she turned to me, her expression a mix of love and determination. "Well, you will all be f***ing going to the funeral, even if I have to carry you all there myself!"

Her tough love was the last thing I wanted to hear in that moment, but somehow it was exactly what I needed. It was a jolt back to reality. Deep down, I knew she was right; this was Richard we were talking about; my husband, our children's father. He deserved to be honoured, to be remembered, and we needed to do that together as a family. The idea of facing the day alone, without Richard, was terrifying, but I realized it was just as important for me and our children to say our final goodbyes with dignity and respect.

That night, after everyone else had gone to bed, I lay awake, the darkness swirling around me. I thought about Richard—his warmth, his laughter, the way he protected me more than I ever realised. I imagined how he would have felt about us avoiding the funeral. He would have wanted us to be there, to embrace the love and support of everyone who had cared for him, and who would continue to care for us.

By morning, I had made up my mind. I would go to the funeral, not just for Richard, but for myself and our children.

March 20, 2013 was the funeral, the second worst day of my life, and only seven days after the worst day of my life. How was I going to do this? How is this my reality now?

I had medication to manage and calm the raw and pure fear I felt going into this day, but I chose not to take it. I knew in my heart and soul that I needed to feel and be present in every agonising emotional moment of Richard's funeral to be able to, in the future, process and heal. I knew that this would eventually be a significant stepping stone in my ability and importance of moving forward.

I felt numb, sick, and overwhelmed with every possible negative emotion that existed. I wanted to dive into the ocean and swim deep under the water so I couldn't hear anything and everything was peaceful.

My children and I walked into Richard's funeral. My head was down. I couldn't look at anyone.

I kissed Richard's mum and twin sister and sat down. That was all I could do.

I didn't notice the casket right in front of us or Richard's surfboard behind it. I didn't notice anyone else in the service. I never looked up the entire service.

I could hear the service commence, but the voices felt so far away.

My oldest sister, Sally, read my eulogy, which I wrote two nights before the funeral with a glass of red wine and then another glass of red wine. I don't know how I wrote it, but I did, and it came from a part of my heart and soul that I didn't even know existed.

Our oldest son, Nicholas, chose to speak at his dad's funeral. I remember him getting up in front of everyone. He couldn't speak. I could hear him trying not to cry, but also quietly sobbing. I couldn't even look up then. I couldn't protect him. I couldn't move.

He had a good friend at the service that was going to stand up with him if he struggled to speak, but he too was in tears.

I'm so proud of what he said standing up there by himself and know what he said had an impact on so many people.

One of Richard's groomsmen at our wedding, Jamie, who was also with us when he passed away, read out a passage from the Bible that was also read at our wedding:

"1 Corinthians 13:13. And now these three remain, Hope, Faith and Love. But the greatest of these is Love."

As stories were shared, laughter intermingled with tears. Each memory painted a vivid picture of Richard, the man we loved, the father who was taken from us too soon. I saw how important it was for the kids to hear those stories, to understand the legacy their father had left behind. It was a chance for them to see that even in his absence, he would always be a part of them.

It wasn't until we came to the part of the service where my family and Richard's family each placed a single red rose on Richard's casket that I actually truly noticed it, which seems unbelievable, I know. The reality of the situation struck me like a tidal wave, pulling me under with a mixture of shock and sorrow. The casket itself was elegantly adorned, with a stunning native and wildflower arrangement that our dear friend Craig had lovingly crafted and gifted. At one end rested Richard's Police Service Hat, a symbol of his dedication and pride in serving his community.

When it was my turn, I stood up and walked slowly toward his casket, each step feeling like it took an eternity. As I placed my rose on the smooth surface, I was beyond numb. This was supposed to be a moment filled with love, but all I could feel was a profound disbelief and soul-destroying sadness. I returned to my seat, focusing on the carpet at my feet, refusing to meet the eyes of others who were doing the same, grappling with their own personal grief and disbelief.

The funeral felt like a surreal dream, as if I were watching from the outside rather than experiencing it fully. More stories were shared, tears flowed, and laughter mingled with the sorrow. Each tribute painted a picture of a man who had lived fiercely and loved deeply, and I found solace in hearing how he had impacted others' lives. But still, the intensity of the finality of it all pressed heavily on my broken and shattered heart

As the service drew to a close, I had made another important decision—one that felt right in my heart. I chose to close the service with a song that resonated deeply with both Richard and me. 'You Raise Me Up' by Josh Groban played, enveloping the room in its powerful melody. If you have a spare couple of minutes to listen to this song, I would truly love for you to do so. For me, it represented the strength that God had given Richard to fight his cancer journey for 21 long years. And now, as I stood there, grappling with my own loss, I felt that this song was also a tribute to my journey—a reminder of that strength I now desperately needed.

As the music swelled, I could feel the love and support of everyone around me, as if we were all united in our grief and loving remembrance. Richard was given a Police Guard of Honour as he left the service, an impressive display of respect and admiration from his colleagues. They stood tall and solemn, saluting him as he made his final journey back to the hearse. My heart swelled with so much love and pride, and in that moment, I realized how much he had meant to so many.

As we followed the procession out of the church, I felt yet another overwhelming wave of emotion. I grasped my children's hands tightly, pulling them close to me. This was our final goodbye, and I wanted to be strong for them, to show them that even in this moment of intensely deep sadness, we could find strength in each other.

Once we reached the hearse, I took a deep breath and glanced at Richard's casket one last time. The world felt incredibly still around me, and I could hear my heart beating in my ears. I wanted to hold onto the memories of our life together, to remember the laughter and the love. This was the man who had fought so hard for us, who had given so much of himself, and I wanted to ensure that his legacy lived on in our hearts and the hearts of his family and friends.

Victoria's words echoed in my mind, and I felt grateful for her insistence. We had faced once again one of our hardest days together, and it was a reminder that sometimes the toughest love is, at times, the most essential, guiding us through our darkest moments.

I didn't and couldn't take in and be wholly present at the time, and I have really appreciated so many friends and family over the years sharing their memories and recollections of Richard's funeral. It's helped me piece together the moments I missed in my daze of grief and disbelief. I was so lost in my own thoughts and feelings that I couldn't truly appreciate the outpouring of love and support surrounding us.

I knew that some friends of Nicholas and Zach's from school were going to be there, but I had no idea that the school had generously provided a bus for their friends and some of the teachers to attend the funeral. It was such a thoughtful and kind gesture, and it warmed my heart to know that the school community had come together to support my boys during such a difficult time.

What I also didn't know was that the Head of Junior School was there, taking Zach and his friends under his wing after the service to make sure they were all doing okay. Bless him! It was comforting to know that the adults in their lives were stepping in, offering guidance and care when I felt utterly overwhelmed. I think it made a world of difference for Zach, who needed that support more than I realised.

The wake was held at a stunning waterfront house belonging to very close friends of ours, Darren and Tracey, in Saratoga. Their house felt like a sanctuary, far removed from the heavy emotions of the day. For a wake I didn't know was coming, didn't know was going to happen, and could in no way have prepared for, it honestly turned out to be perfect.

Our friends had gone to incredible lengths to create a welcoming environment. The house was beautifully decorated, the setting was serene, and the food was plentiful and delicious, thanks to the generosity of other friends who gifted us the catering, Paul and Kate. Their thoughtfulness and support truly shone through, wrapping us in warmth during this hard and challenging time.

As I stood there, surrounded by family and friends, I felt a bittersweet mix of emotions wash over me. While the day had been so tragic and heartbreaking, it also became an unexpected comfort sharing this precious time with our family and friends that knew and loved Richard. People gathered in small groups, sharing stories and reminiscing about the good and special times they had with Richard, and I could see and feel the love and respect they had for him. There was something comforting about hearing those stories, knowing that Richard had left a lasting impact on so many lives.

I watched as Emily, Nicholas and Zach connected with their friends. They needed that support now more than ever, and seeing them sharing memories and even laughing sometimes, reminded me of the bond they all shared. It brought a small smile to my face amid the overwhelming sadness.

As the sun began to set over the water, casting a beautiful, golden glow on everything around us, I felt a moment of clarity. I realised that while Richard was no longer physically with us, he was very much present in our hearts and in the love we were surrounded by. His spirit lived on through our shared memories, the stories being told, and the love that enveloped us.

That day was a testament to the community we had around us—a network of friends and family who were ready to stand by our side, offering support and understanding as we navigated this new reality. It was a small reminder that even in our darkest moments, we were not alone. Together, we would find a way to honour Richard's legacy and carry his love forward in our lives.

The house, the setting, the food, our family and friends– It was a beautiful ending to a truly tragic, heartbreaking, unbearable, and soul-destroying day.

Family

Chapter Eight

Grief

I'm writing this chapter entirely from my own experience. I'm not an expert in grief; I can only share what I have felt and what I have gone through. Grief is so personal and unique to each of us. There is no right or wrong way to grieve, but I firmly believe that your grief, whatever form it takes, is right for you. It's messy, raw, sometimes unbearable, and unpredictable. So, while it may not always be pretty, what I'm sharing is real.

When we left the ICU late that Wednesday afternoon, after saying our final goodbyes to Richard, I was handed the Traumatic Death Folder. It was thick, filled with paperwork I couldn't even look at, let alone open. It felt cold and impersonal. The name alone—*Traumatic Death Folder*—was a reminder of the unbearable reality I now had to face. How was this real? How had this become my life? I brought it home and left it untouched for a long time. I wasn't ready. But eventually, I did open it. I'll get to that later.

That first evening home, we arrived late in the day. It was a blur. I remember feeling again like I was watching myself from the outside, completely numb. My body was exhausted beyond comprehension, yet my mind was racing uncontrollably. I felt sick, like the weight of everything was physically pressing down on me. And the tears (oh, the tears) wouldn't stop, even though I felt too tired to cry. They burned my face, and my eyes were so sore, like crying vinegar. The sobs came in waves, and when I wasn't crying, I just sat there in stunned silence.

On the drive home, I suddenly remembered that Richard had some leftover Valium from his treatments. I don't know why it popped into my mind at that moment, but it did. It was like an escape route, a brief relief from the pain I couldn't bear to feel. That night, after the kids had gone to bed, I poured myself a vodka, grabbed the Valium, and downed it. For the next month, this became my nightly ritual.

I'm not proud of it, but I also don't judge myself for it now. Grief takes you to places you never thought you'd go, and this was where I found myself. The Valium and vodka became the only way I could numb the unbearable reality of losing Richard, and the only way to stop my mind at night enough to be able to fall asleep. As the days went on, the VV, double V (as I called it in my head) turned into VVV; triple V, Valium and *double* vodka. Because, let's face it, after the days I was enduring, one vodka wasn't going to cut it. I needed something stronger to dull the edge, to stop the thoughts and feelings from overwhelming me.

I knew, though, deep down, that I couldn't rely on the Valium forever. As a Registered Nurse, I was all too aware of how quickly addiction could creep up, and I didn't want to add that battle to everything else I was dealing with. After a month of this self-medicating routine, I decided to wean myself off the Valium. It wasn't easy, but I was determined.

The vodka, however, was another story. I didn't stop that. In fact, some nights, it wasn't just two drinks, it was more. I needed it, or at least that's what I told myself. It helped me get through the long, lonely nights when the weight of grief felt unbearable, when I didn't know how to face another day without Richard by my side.

Looking back now, I see that I was just trying to survive. I had to find a way to make it through those first few weeks, months and even years, and that's what I did. It wasn't healthy, but it was what I knew how to do at the time. Grief doesn't come with a manual, and sometimes you just have to do whatever it takes to keep putting one foot in front of the other.

I wasn't ready to face the world without him, and I wasn't ready to feel the full force of my grief. The Valium, the vodka, the numbness. It was my way of avoiding the unbearable truth that Richard was gone.

I didn't know how to grieve the sudden, indescribable, and soul-destroying death of Richard. I remember desperately wanting a manual or a book that would tell me *how* to do this, step by step, because I had no idea how to get through it. I felt completely lost. If such a book had existed, I would have followed it to the letter.

In the weeks following his death, the fog of disbelief still hung heavy over me. But eventually, one day I opened the Traumatic Death Folder. It was overwhelming, filled with information I couldn't fully comprehend in my broken state, but there were two key pieces of advice that I clung to, like a lifeline in the middle of a storm.

1) Never stop talking about the person who has died. Even though it feels painful, especially in those early days, weeks, and months, keeping their memory alive through conversation is important. Every day, I spoke about Richard. Every day, it felt like ripping open the wound again and again, and it broke my heart a little more each time.

I also distinctly remember making the decision never to play the 'victim' role at any time after Richard died, nor did I ever let our children do this. It's definitely not to say that without doubt we all at times could have played that role a million times over, but 12 years on, my heart is at peace that we didn't.

We still talk about Richard all the time. We can now smile, laugh, and reminisce about the good times, the precious moments we shared with him. There's absolutely healing in keeping his memory alive, even when it felt so incredibly hard at first.

2) Let your children see you cry, hurt, and grieve. My instinct as a parent was to shield our kids from my pain. I wanted to protect them from seeing me fall apart. But that advice stuck with me, and I realised they *needed* to see me go through this. They needed to see me cry, to witness my raw, unfiltered grief. Because they then also needed to see that, eventually, I could stop crying. That I could pick myself up, start to heal, and find a way forward. Showing them my grief wasn't a sign of weakness, but a necessary step in showing them that it's okay to feel, to hurt, to grieve and to eventually start to heal.

Three weeks after Richard's death, when I thought the grief could get no worse, I received a phone call that shattered what was left of me. I had thought I was already living the worst version of reality, but this took me to a place of pain and despair I didn't know existed. My world crumbled, again. The ground beneath me gave way, the sky fell in, and I was plunged into a darkness I could never have imagined.

What came next was another excruciating decision I had to make. I had to, choose to, and needed to be the one to tell Emily and Nicholas the truth about their dad's death. It was a truth I never wanted to hear or wanted to speak, a burden

I didn't want to place on their young shoulders. But I couldn't bear the thought of someone else telling them. As their mum, I felt it was my cross to bear. I had to be the one to sit quietly and tell them, no matter how unbearable it was. It was one of the hardest things I've ever done. I didn't want to say the words, but they had to hear them from me.

Zach was only 10 years old at the time. He was too young, too fragile, to carry that truth. Losing his dad was more than enough for him to deal with at such a tender age. I made the decision to wait. I chose not to tell him until he was 16, when I felt he might be able to better process it. It was a decision I agonised over, but I knew it was the right one for him. Even then, when the time finally came to tell him, it was just as devastating. But it was the only way I knew how to protect him from a grief that could have broken him too soon.

Those weeks were filled with a pain I can't fully describe. I felt like I was falling through an endless void, one that was dark, frightening, unpredictable and suffocating. Every step, every conversation, felt like dragging myself through quicksand. I was barely holding on, but somehow, I kept going. I don't know how, but I did. I knew if I stopped holding my head above water, stopped swimming as exhaustingly hard as it was, that I would probably take everyone down with me. I wanted to stop swimming so hard so many times, it would definitely have been the easier way out for me, but by the Grace of God I kept swimming as hard as I could.

Some days, I would tell myself, *'Just get through the next minute.'* But, even that often felt like too much, so I would cut it down to just 30 seconds. That was about as much as I could bear to keep focusing on - getting through 30 seconds of grief, then another, and then another. It was my way of coping with the enormity of the loss I was feeling.

I wasn't only trying to manage my own grief, but also the grief of my children. And we were all grieving in different ways. It wasn't always pretty, far from it. In fact, it was messy and raw, and I often found myself wondering how on earth I was supposed to handle it all. How could I, when I felt like I had lost my identity and half of my being?

I remember thinking I would never smile again. And on the rare occasions when I did, usually by accident, I was consumed by guilt. How could I smile when Richard was gone? How could I even think about being happy, eating a nice meal, or enjoying a moment of peace after everything that had happened to him? It seemed wrong to even consider that there might still be some joy in the world. But at the same time, I was exhausted from trying to be strong, from trying to hold myself together when I felt shattered into thousands of pieces.

I felt like I should have been strong enough to handle it all, to deal with the trauma of losing my husband and father of our children. But in reality, I wasn't. And you know what? That's OK. I've come to understand that there's no 'right' way to cope with something so devastating. Sometimes you can't be strong, and that's absolutely fine. Grief strips you down to your most vulnerable state, and I had to learn that it was OK not to be ok, not to have all the answers or to always keep it together.

One of the best decisions I made was going on antidepressants, with the help of my wonderfully supportive GP. For me, they were a lifeline and pivotal turning point. There's often a stigma around this medication, but I'm a huge advocate for it now. Antidepressants helped my brain reconnect and start mending the broken pathways that trauma had severed. I felt like they gave me a chance to breathe again, to lift the weight just enough so I could begin to function effectively again. They weren't a magic cure, but they were a vital part of my healing, and I can honestly say they were life changing and life saving for me. Whether you need them for six months, a year, or longer, there's no shame at all in needing that extra help for however long.

Another crucial lesson I learned was the importance of asking for help. For so long, I thought I should be strong enough to handle everything on my own. I didn't want to burden others with my grief, and I certainly didn't want to ask for anything. But I wasn't strong enough on my own, and that's OK too. What surprised me the most was that the world didn't fall apart when I asked for help. It didn't spin off its axis just because I needed support. In fact, I discovered that people *wanted* to help. They also needed to, in some way, because it helped them cope with their own grief. They felt like they were doing something, and that mattered to them as much as it did to me.

The kindness and generosity we received in those early months was overwhelming. For the first six months after Richard passed away, I didn't have to cook a single meal for my family. Our church, our children's school, and the local community rallied around us. Every night, without fail, someone would drop off a homemade dinner. It was an incredible gift, not just because it lifted the burden of having to think about shopping and cooking, but because it reminded me that we weren't alone in our grief. People were with us, supporting us, carrying us through in ways both big and small.

It was humbling, to say the least, and I learnt to accept that help, even when it felt hard to do so. Looking back, those acts of kindness were part of what kept us going through those darkest days.

It was also during this dark and overwhelming time that I finally put my hand up and said, "I need professional help." My grief was all-consuming, a constant weight that I couldn't lift. Watching my children grieve, each in their own way, was unbearable. I couldn't eat. I couldn't sleep. I had no idea how to keep living in a world that I had been so cruelly, heartlessly, and violently thrown into. It wasn't just a case of falling into grief; I felt as though I'd been *slam dunked* into it, with no way out.

Making the decision to see a psychologist was one of the best things I could have done for myself. It was a turning point, a lifeline, that helped me slowly begin to piece together the many shattered parts of my life. At first, I felt guilty for needing help. After all, I was a mum. I was supposed to be strong, wasn't I? But I came to realise that seeking help was a strength in itself.

For the first six months after Richard's death, I blamed myself to the core of my being. I carried this unbearable weight of guilt as a Registered Nurse. How could I not have known what was happening to Richard? How could I have failed to save him? These thoughts plagued me every second of every day. The self-blame was relentless, gnawing away at any chance of possible healing.

When I finally voiced these thoughts in my sessions with my psychologist, she helped me begin to unpack this overwhelming guilt. Gently, rationally, she talked me through it. She explained how irrational and unrealistic my self-blame was, reminding me that even as a nurse, I was still just human. The way she spoke to me, it wasn't clinical or detached. It was kind, empathetic, and full of understanding. And for the first time, I felt the weight of the world lift, just a little. It was as though I'd been given permission to grieve without guilt. And that small but significant shift allowed me to start healing in a far healthier, more realistic way.

But as time went on, I encountered another obstacle: *forgiveness*. How was I ever going to forgive what happened to Richard? I knew deep down that holding on to anger, hurt, and blame wasn't healthy. I knew that it wasn't conducive to my healing. But I simply didn't know how to let go of these emotions or where to even start finding forgiveness.

My psychologist, in her gentle and wise way, suggested something that felt like another revelation: maybe no one needed or wanted my forgiveness. Maybe I didn't have to rush into forgiving anyone for now. It was like another burden had been lifted. She gave me permission to shelve those feelings for the time being and focus on simply grieving. I didn't need to force forgiveness right away, if ever. I could just *be* in my grief without having to tick all the boxes of what I thought healing should look like.

I saw my psychologist for about a year after Richard's death. And during that time, her office became a safe space where I could lay bare the rawness of my grief, my anger, my guilt, and my confusion. If those walls could talk, they would tell stories of deep pain, but also of the slow, tentative steps toward healing. There were days I would sit in that chair and cry until I couldn't breathe. Other days I would just sit there, feeling numb, with nothing to say. But through it all, I was rebuilding.

After about a year of endlessly replaying the 'what ifs', 'if onlys', 'it should have' and 'it could have' in my head and in every conversation; "If only the transplant had gone differently... he shouldn't have died... Richard should still be here." My psychologist finally stopped me in my tracks. I think she had been waiting for the right moment to tell me what I needed to hear, even though it would be hard to accept.

She told me, bluntly but kindly, that I needed to stop living in a past-tense universe that I had created, one where everything unfolded differently. A world that didn't exist. She said, "It's time to live in the reality where *it has happened, it did happen, and he very sadly isn't here anymore.*"

That was a real turning point. It felt like a 'bitch slap', as I've come to call it, harsh but necessary. And she was right. I had been stuck in a loop, living in a fantasy where I could rewrite the past, constantly torturing myself with a version of reality that didn't and couldn't exist. From that moment, I made a conscious effort to stop doing this. Every time I caught myself saying, "He should still be here," I would pull myself back to the present.

It wasn't easy, not by any means. That fantasy world was where my grief found a strange kind of comfort. It was a place where I could *almost* imagine Richard still with us. But as painful as it was, learning to live in the reality of his death was crucial. It was a significant step toward moving forward, though that didn't mean 'moving on' from Richard or forgetting him at all. It just meant learning how to navigate life without him in a more real, grounded way.

There was another moment, deeply etched in my memory, that I continue to struggle with to this day. It happened the day Richard died, and it's one of those unforgiving moments that plays over and over in my mind.

Zach was standing at the foot of Richard's bed in the ICU when the doctors told us they were going to stop all life-supporting treatment. Quietly, they'd told me that it wouldn't be long before Richard passed away. As I lay there, my head on Richard's chest, I could see Zach standing alone, crying at the end of the bed. He looked so small, so vulnerable, standing there by himself, his face pale and terrified.

I asked him to come up and be with me, or to join Emily, Nicholas, and Richard's mum who were on the other side of the bed. But he shook his head, his tears streaming down, too overwhelmed to move. My heart broke seeing him standing there, isolated in his grief. It felt so wrong, so agonising, that I couldn't let him stay there on his own. I lifted my head from Richard's chest, just for a moment, and went to Zach.

I wrapped my arms around him, trying to offer him whatever comfort I could muster in that unbearable moment. I begged him to come up to where we were, so I could return to Richard's side while he was still alive, but Zach couldn't move. He was paralysed by the weight of what was happening. I was torn between comforting my 10 year old son and wanting to be back with Richard as he slipped away.

I choose to leave Zach and lay back on Richard's chest as he passed away.

This is one of those moments that haunts me still. I wanted to be in two places at once, and no matter what I did, I felt like I was failing. Failing Richard by not being there at the end, and failing Zach by not doing enough to protect him from the pain of watching his father die. That impossible choice, being with my son or being with my husband, still lingers in my heart. Even now, I wrestle with it, wondering if I made the right decision in those final moments.

But grief is complicated, and it comes with a thousand tiny moments of doubt, regret, and second-guessing. Slowly, I've come to realise that there was no right or wrong in that situation. I did the best I could, given the overwhelming weight of it all. I was trying to hold both my son and my husband in that unbearable moment of loss. It doesn't make the memory any less painful, but it has helped me find a little more compassion for myself. I was, after all, grieving too.

Approximately four years later, during a crucial appointment with a forensic psychiatrist, I brought up that agonising moment, the one where I left Richard's side to comfort Zach at the end of his bed. I spoke about the unrelenting guilt and the struggle to forgive myself, feeling as though I had somehow let Zach down and not been there for him when I left him to go back to be with Richard.

Her response was simple, but profound. She said, "But maybe that was exactly where he wanted and needed to be, and it was right for him." That one sentence gave me a sense of release. It allowed me to start forgiving myself, even if only a little. Maybe Zach standing there, lost in his grief, could undoubtedly see the love of his mum and dad.

As a Registered Nurse, I had learned about the five stages of grief—denial, anger, bargaining, depression, and acceptance. What I didn't know, and what no one teaches you, is that grief isn't a linear process. After you've gone through those stages, you don't tick them off a list and move on. You revisit them, over and over again, at different times and in different ways. Even now, I find myself grappling with some of those stages all over again.

In that first year following Richard's death, I actually and honestly believed that somehow, he would come back. Every single day, I thought if I thought hard enough, I could somehow reverse or go back in time and stop any of this from happening.

I know it sounds insane, but I honestly believed in my heart I could do this. It was emotionally and mentally exhausting, on top of already being emotionally, mentally, and physically exhausted.

The kids school also, had offered at this time, to landscape the front and back garden of our house, and my immediate instinct was to say no. I felt uncomfortable accepting such a big gesture, as though I should somehow be handling things on my own, even though I clearly wasn't. But then, I stopped myself. This was another example of people wanting to help, to do something kind for us, and I had to learn to graciously and humbly accept their offer.

And I'm so glad I did. The team of students and teachers who came to our home were incredible. They poured their hearts into transforming our garden, and the result was nothing short of amazing. Every time I looked outside, I was reminded of the love and care that our community had shown us during such a painful and difficult time. It wasn't just about the landscaping; it was about people showing up for us in ways I never expected. I was beyond thankful and appreciative for the time, effort, and energy they all put in.

The garden became a peaceful place for us, a place of quiet reflection and even healing. It wasn't just a physical transformation of the space, it was a symbolic gesture of growth and renewal. It's strange, but sometimes in the middle of grief, when everything feels so dark and heavy, these unexpected moments of light come through. The garden became one of those for us, and our new 8-week-old cocker spaniel puppy, Daisy.

I realised that by allowing people to help, I was letting them be part of our journey, part of our healing. It wasn't just about us; it was about the connections we had built over the years, and how those connections were now supporting us when we needed them most. Letting people in wasn't a sign of weakness, it was an acknowledgment of the strength that comes from community, from leaning on others when you can't stand on your own.

Looking at that garden, I felt humbled. It was a reminder that, even in our most difficult times, we're not as alone as we sometimes felt. And accepting help doesn't take anything away from your strength. Instead, it adds to it in ways you might not immediately see.

That first year was filled with so much darkness and uncertainty. I couldn't imagine feeling any other way, let alone being able to look forward to the future. But now, I can say that while the grief is still there, it no longer defines me. It's become part of my story, part of who I am, but it's not the only story I have to tell.

Richard in his element

Chapter Nine

Triggers

Triggers come in the forms of Christmases, birthdays, anniversaries, and major life events. Each milestone, whether it's a birth, a death, a marriage, or even a small achievement, can bring grief rushing back, sometimes catching me completely off guard. The difference now is that these feelings are less frequent, less suffocating, and less unbearable than they once were.

I used to hate the saying 'time heals all wounds.' When Richard first passed away, that phrase would make me angry. How could time ever heal something so raw and devastating? I truly felt in my soul that I would always carry that overwhelming sadness, that I would never feel okay again. But over time, I've learned that while time doesn't necessarily *heal* all wounds, it does *soften* them. The sharp edges of grief become smoother, less painful to touch. The rawness of the emotion fades, and though the scar remains, it no longer consumes me the way it once did. By the grace of God, the intensity has lessened and eased.

I remember thinking at the time, "Am I going to feel like this forever? How will I ever stop feeling this crushing weight and intensity of sadness and despair?" It seemed impossible to imagine that anything could ever change. Yet slowly, with the help of time, family, friends, my faith, therapy, medication, and an incredibly strong and loving support network, the hopelessness started to shift.

Grief doesn't have an end date. It's not something you 'get over' or 'move on' from, but it does evolve. I've come to realise and embrace that it's okay to feel moments of joy again, to laugh, to find happiness without feeling guilty. It doesn't mean I've forgotten Richard or what we went through, it just means I'm learning to live with my grief in a way that allows me to still live.

On the first anniversary of Richard's death, after having been through a year of 'firsts', I had decided to spend that day and the next at a hotel in Sydney that we held fond memories of: the Shangri-La. We always enjoyed our time there.

Here's where I start heading down a massive rabbit hole. For the first time ever, I actually wanted to feel sorry for myself. I wanted to have a pity party, and I wanted to let myself feel everything I had been so desperately trying not to feel, in all its exposing and primal rawness.

I took two movies to watch - The Notebook and P.S. I Love You - and a lot of alcohol.

Most people I had told what I was planning to do on that anniversary date didn't think it was a good idea, particularly to be by myself, which I didn't understand at the time. I just knew in my heart that I wanted to and needed to do this.

My psychologist asked me, and rightly so in hindsight, if I had access to a firearm. I did not, nor was I going down that pathway, but obviously she and other people did think that, and I truly am thankful that they spoke up and voiced their concerns.

When I walked into that hotel room and stood there, gazing out over the sparkling waters of Sydney Harbour, the weight of that truth crashed down on me. The beauty of the view contrasted sharply with the painful heaviness in my heart. I had tried so hard to avoid this moment, to protect myself from the pain of truly accepting the loss, but now it was unavoidable. Richard was not coming back. The reality of it felt like yet another tsunami, sweeping over me and threatening to pull me under. I allowed myself to be overwhelmed by the grief I had been holding at bay for far too long.

I sank onto the plush carpet, clutching Richard's Funeral Guest Register in my hands I had brought with me and had never looked at. It was filled with names and messages of love and support, each one a reminder of the connections

Richard had forged in his life. I traced the handwritten notes with my fingers, reading the words over and over. Some expressed condolences, others shared cherished memories, and some simply offered words of encouragement. Each message was a lifeline, but they also cut so deep, a painful reminder of what I had lost.

Then there were the sympathy cards. I had put them into a drawer, unable to confront the emotional weight they carried. But now, sitting in that room, I felt ready to face them. I opened one after another, letting the words wash over me. Tears streamed down my face as I read heartfelt messages that spoke of love, memories, and the profound impact Richard had on so many lives. The tears came in waves, each card prompting a fresh rush of emotion, a mixture of sorrow, gratitude, and longing.

Finally, it was time to indulge in the movies I had brought with me. I knew I was choosing films known for their heart-wrenching themes of love and loss, but I craved that catharsis. I curled up on the hotel bed with a blanket and a glass of wine, allowing myself to sink into the stories. As the characters navigated their grief, I felt an overwhelming sense of companionship in my sorrow. I cried freely, releasing pent-up emotions that had been bottled inside me this last year.

I reflected on the past year, the 'firsts' I had experienced without Richard; the first birthdays, the first holiday, the first anniversary of our wedding. Each moment had felt like a dagger through my heart, and now, on this anniversary, I finally allowed myself to acknowledge the depth of that pain. I wanted to grieve not just for Richard but for the life we had shared, the dreams we had for our future and the little everyday moments that now felt achingly absent.

In that hotel room, with the intensity of my grief on my shoulders and a glass of wine in hand, I felt the need to be raw and vulnerable. I gave myself permission to feel sorry for myself, to acknowledge my loneliness and soul-destroying sadness, and to let the tears flow. For the first time in a long time, I didn't feel the need to put on a brave face or pretend everything was okay. I was simply allowed to *be*.

I often found myself crying in the shower. There was something oddly comforting about the way the warm water enveloped me, as if my tears became part of the stream, blending into the flow and making the sadness feel a little less heavy. Sometimes, I wished I could just stay in there forever, letting the water wash away not only my tears but also the pain that lingered in my heart.

But on this particular day, I opted for a relaxing bubble bath instead. I thought it might help me unwind and settle my mind a little, if only for a moment. As I sank into the warm water, the sound of my sobs filled the bathroom. The raw and literal agonising emotion that came out of me was cathartic, a release I desperately needed. I was utterly exhausted physically, emotionally and mentally, and as strange as it may sound, I finally felt a sense of relief wash over me. It was the undeniable realisation that Richard truly wasn't coming back.

I could finally stop fighting with every fiber of my being to somehow bring Richard back.

As the sun began to set, casting a warm golden glow across the water, I looked out at the horizon, where the sky met the sea. It was beautiful, yet haunting. In that moment, I felt a connection to Richard, a sense that he was there with me, encouraging and helping me to accept my grief rather than push it down, hide from or deny it. I thought of all the times we had spent together in that hotel, laughing and enjoying life. And now, I understood that it was okay to be sad. It was okay to miss him, to wish he were still here, and to feel the weight of that absence in my heart.

That night, I completely surrendered to my emotions, letting them wash over me like cleansing rain. The pity party I had longed for was not about wallowing; it was about honouring my feelings and acknowledging the journey I had been on. I went to bed that night feeling both shattered and exhausted, but strangely a little lighter, ready to face the next day, the anniversary of Richard's death.

That day, I met our children and Richard's mum for lunch in Manly on the anniversary of his passing. It was a heart-breaking affair. None of us wanted to be there, but we felt we had to do something to acknowledge the day, and at the very least just be there for each other and with each other. The weight of loss, sadness and heartbreak hung over us, and I found myself wishing for the 24 hours of 13 March, 2014 to just hurry up and be over, it was agonizing.

For as long as I can remember, I have always felt a deep instinct about what to do at certain moments, guided by my heart. I had decided to divide Richard's ashes into three urns, and on this first anniversary, I wanted to scatter a third of them at Clontarf Beach in Middle Harbour. This beach held so many memories for us - growing up there, spending sunny afternoons with family and friends, and sharing moments of pure happiness and joy. Richard and his twin sister had even sailed and raced on those waters in their youth.

Only our children and Richard's immediate family knew when and where we were going to do this. It felt right to keep it intimate, a moment just for us to honour Richard in a place filled with love and memories. The anticipation of that moment filled me with a bittersweet sense of peace, even amidst the heartache.

It was early April, right around Easter, when Richard's twin sister, Sarah, had come over from New Zealand. It was so important to me that as many of Richard's immediate family members as possible could be there for this moment.

We all felt a deep need to be together, to honour him collectively.

By around 4 PM, we found ourselves at the far end of Clontarf Beach. The sun was beginning to dip towards the horizon, casting a beautiful shine over the water. We had decided that each of us would take a turn sharing a memory of Richard before scattering some of his ashes into the water. The air was heavy with emotion, a mix of grief and gratitude as we recounted the moments we cherished with him.

As we began our tribute to Richard, I noticed a man swimming with his dog in the distance. I felt a pang of anxiety, hoping he wouldn't swim down as far as we were. It seemed awkward to think he might stumble upon our intimate moment, especially given the emotional importance of what we were doing.

One by one, we shared our memories, each heartfelt word echoing our love for Richard. It felt both beautiful and heartbreaking, as if we were weaving a tapestry of our collective grief. As we took our turns scattering his ashes into his beloved Middle Harbour, the waves seemed to gently embrace them, carrying our love into the depths of the water.

However, the swimmer and his dog were getting closer, and I realised he was undoubtedly headed straight for the ashes we had just scattered. My heart raced. I braced myself for an awkward encounter, wondering how he would react to swimming into, realizing and witnessing our mourning.

The man swam up to where we all were and stood up in the water. I caught a glimpse of his face and noticed tears streaming down his cheeks. Why was he crying? Did he know what we were doing? My mind raced, trying to place him, but I couldn't recognise him.

As he walked toward us, everything suddenly became clear. It was Richard's friend Greg, the very same Greg whose house I had first met Richard at! I was in disbelief. What were the odds? It felt incredibly surreal.

Greg had been an old neighbour of Richard's family, and he knew all of them well. In that moment, it felt like somehow he was absolutely meant to be there. He brought a comforting presence in an intimately private outpouring of our personal grief. More tears flowed, but they were joined by hugs and love. What an astonishingly precious moment in time!

In the midst of our sorrow, there was a familiar face, a shared connection to Richard, reminding us that love and memories endure beyond loss. We embraced Greg tightly, grateful for his unexpected presence. It felt like Richard himself was present in that moment, uniting us in our shared grief and love and our journey of healing and moving forward.

I could see that Zach was struggling on this day. There was so much for an eleven-year-old to process, and I wished I could take away his pain. He had found a small lead fishing sinker on the beach, with some fishing line still attached. He picked it up and began to play with it, twisting and turning it between his fingers. I could see how much it distracted him from the reality of what we were all doing. To this day, he still keeps that sinker, a tangible reminder of that bittersweet moment.

As the second anniversary of Richard's passing approached, I felt a deep sense of purpose again about how I wanted to honour him. Richard had spent countless hours surfing with a close-knit group of mates who affectionately called themselves 'The Pod'.

Early that morning, 'The Pod' and their families gathered on the beach at Wamberal, one of Richard's favourite surfing spots. The sun was just beginning to rise, casting a warm glow over the water, and the salty breeze carried with it a sense of camaraderie and remembrance. It felt right to be there, surrounded by so much love.

As we gathered in a circle on the sand, I invited anyone who wanted to share a few words about Richard to do so. One by one, they spoke, their voices cracking with emotion as they recounted the memories they held dear. Each story painted a vivid picture of Richard's spirit, his laughter, his kindness, his friendship, his faith and his undeniable passion for life.

After the tributes, my boys, 'The Pod', and some of their children paddled out past the break, forming a Circle of Honour. As they sat there on their boards, a sense of unity enveloped us all. It felt like Richard again was right there with us, watching over this moment, being with us through our grief.

As they scattered Richard's ashes into the shimmering water, something remarkable happened. At that very moment, a pod of dolphins breached out of the water, right next to 'The Pod' and their Circle of Honour. It was a goosebump moment, a perfect and beautiful reminder of what Richard had meant to us all.

The sight was breathtaking, the dolphins dancing through the waves, their sleek bodies glistening in the sunlight. I couldn't help but feel that Richard was without doubt with us at this moment, his presence, his love, and his unwavering spirit.

Twelve years on, I have navigated the emotional landscape of grieving Richard's absence - at our oldest son, Nicholas's wedding, and the births of our three precious and beautiful grandchildren. And will again at our daughter's wedding in November this year. Each milestone serves as a bittersweet reminder of what could have been. It was a life lost and memories that will never be created. The thought that Richard never got to meet his grandchildren, witness their first steps, or be part of our family's happy and joyful moments weighs heavily on my heart. It's a deep ache, a constant reminder of an integral part of our lives taken from us too soon.

The pain cuts even deeper when I think about our daughter Emily. Knowing that Richard will never walk our daughter down the aisle on her wedding day fills me with indescribable sorrow. It's a moment that will forever be stolen from her, from us, a cherished tradition that will remain unfulfilled. As a mother, I feel it's my duty to ensure that this moment, though altered by loss, will still be a precious and meaningful moment in time. I promise you Emily that you will never walk that path alone. It would be an honour and a privilege to stand beside you, representing your dad as you embark on this new chapter of your life. I know her brothers would feel exactly the same way, and we will all be there for you, holding you up in the absence of the man who would have been so proud.

It's important for me to acknowledge that it's okay not to be okay. It's okay to feel sorry for yourself and to allow yourself to grieve. It's okay to go down that rabbit hole of despair, just don't stay there! I have learned that while it's important to give yourself permission to feel these emotions, it's equally important to find a way to emerge from them.

In my journey, I made a promise to myself: I would allow these 'dark hours' to exist, but only for a certain amount of time, usually 12 hours. This self-imposed limit became a lifeline, a way to navigate the storm of grief without becoming overwhelmed. I would set a timer, and during that time, I would allow myself to feel every ounce of sadness, anger, and confusion. I would cry, scream, and let it all out. But once that timer went off, I would take a deep breath and remind myself to shift my focus, to take another step forward.

I truly believe that if you deny yourself these feelings or suppress them at all costs, you hinder your ability to progress in your grieving process. Embracing the pain has become a necessary part of healing. I've learned that allowing these emotions to surface, though uncomfortable, enables me to process my grief in a healthier way. It's a balancing act, but it's one I continue to navigate as I honour Richard's memory and the love we shared.

As time goes on, I find strength not only in my memories of Richard but in the love and support of my family. Each anniversary, each milestone, reminds me of the importance of holding onto those memories while also forging new ones. I have learned to find joy again amidst the sorrow, to celebrate the life we had, and to carry Richard's spirit with us as we continue to create our own stories and move forward with our lives without him.

'The Pod'

Chapter Ten

Rollercoasters

I returned to work as a Surgical Registered Nurse three months after Richard passed away. It was a daunting and very overwhelming decision, but I chose to go back to the ten night shifts I was familiar with— a job and routine I knew well and could depend on during such a tumultuous time.

My work family welcomed me back with open arms, providing a level of support that was nothing short of extraordinary. They were compassionate, empathetic, and unwavering in their love and encouragement, offering me a sense of stability when everything else in my life felt uncertain. Their kindness gave me strength to take the first steps back into a profession that had been my cornerstone for so many years.

Returning to work, however, was far from easy. Looking after critically ill and dying patients in the wake of my own profound loss was emotionally taxing. But at that point in my life, it was all I knew how to do. My world had been turned upside down, and I lacked the capacity to make significant changes or even contemplate an alternative path.

Financially, I was unsure where I stood. My immediate focus was on ensuring there was food on the table for my children and that the bills were paid. The practicalities of life loomed large, forcing me to push through the pain of working at a challenging job and focus on survival.

From the very first night I returned though, my journey back to work took an unexpected and deeply troubling turn. A male colleague, someone I had worked alongside for years and considered a friend, began to treat me with hostility and disgust. He bullied, intimidated, and harassed me, creating a toxic environment that made an already difficult situation unbearable. It felt like having to work in a domestic violence environment when I was rostered on with him, which was often.

I filed numerous written complaints and participated in several meetings to address his behaviour. Despite these efforts, his actions continued unabated, leaving me feeling increasingly belittled and distressed.

The situation escalated during a hospital mediation meeting when he made outrageous and false accusations against me. He claimed that I had been filing secret complaints about him, stalking him in various places, including following him into the bathroom, to his home in the mornings, to the shops where I allegedly waited for him in the car park, and even on his family holiday. He asserted that he had photographic evidence of me and my car.

To make matters worse, he also alleged that all this information was with his lawyer and that there was a 'plan in place' for me. These accusations were completely baseless and untrue but hearing them was deeply confronting and concerning.

When I returned home that day, I was overwhelmed with fear and disbelief. Feeling incredibly rattled and unsure of what to do, I reached out to a police friend of Richard's, Adam, to share with him what had happened and voice my concerns. His advice was clear and immediate: go to the local police station and make an official report about the events that transpired during the mediation meeting. Following his guidance, I filed the report, hoping it would provide some form of protection and a record of the ordeal I was enduring.

My colleague's relentless campaign of harassment continued for an exhausting five years. It became a shadow that loomed over every aspect of my work life, leaving me constantly on edge and deeply eroded my sense of safety and self-worth.

By January 2018, the physical and emotional toll of this and other prolonged stressors was manifesting in ways I could no longer ignore. One afternoon, after a particularly busy day, I lay down to have a rest before another long night shift. Sleep evaded me; my heart felt as though it was racing uncontrollably, and a deep, radiating pain coursed through both my ears and down my neck. It wasn't just discomfort—it was something I had never felt before.

Frustrated by my inability to relax and sleep for a little while, I decided to get up and make a coffee, hoping it would energise me and shake off whatever strange sensation I was experiencing. The moment I stood up though, I was hit by a wave of dizziness so severe I could not stand upright. It was as if the world had tilted on its axis, and I had no choice but to collapse back onto the bed.

At first, I dismissed it as an isolated incident, maybe I got up too fast or just being overly tired. I tried standing up again, determined to shake it off, but the same overwhelming dizziness and inability to stand upright hit me with brutal force. Feeling confused but still not overly alarmed, I thought, *a strong cup of coffee is all I need to snap out of this.*

Crawling out of bed—because walking wasn't an option—I made my way to the kitchen, brewed myself a double shot of coffee, and crawled back to my bed to drink it. Surely, this would set me right.

After finishing the coffee, I attempted to stand up again, only to find that the symptoms had not improved. In fact, they had intensified. The dizziness, coupled with a crippling sensation I couldn't quite describe, was now completely debilitating. I could barely process what was happening to my body, let alone why.

Feeling desperate and out of options, I called out to my youngest son, Zach, who was 16 at the time. I asked him, with no real plan in mind, whether he'd come with me if I drove myself to the hospital. Looking back, I can't imagine what I was thinking—I could barely stand, let alone drive a car.

Zach walked into my room, took one look at me, and immediately said, "I think you need to call an ambulance." His calm but firm statement made sense on some level, but I stubbornly resisted the idea. I didn't want to cause a fuss or admit that I was incapable of managing this on my own. Ambulances were for emergencies—surely, this wasn't *that*.

But as I lay there, struggling to sit up and realising how seriously Zach was taking the situation, I began to question whether I might need to reconsider.

We had only been in our new home for a few months, and the thought of an ambulance arriving and me being stretchered out in full view of the neighbours was unthinkable. Pride and stubbornness won the day, and Zach and I reached a compromise. Instead of calling an ambulance, I ordered an Uber.

When the Uber arrived, I mustered every ounce of strength and composure to walk out to the car. The driver's expression said it all—he looked utterly terrified. Whether it was the emergency department destination or the sight of me barely holding it together, I'll never know. To this day, I maintain that I appeared much more collected than I probably felt, so I like to think his concern was more about the destination than me.

Once we were on our way, Zach, ever the opportunist, decided it was the perfect time to lighten the mood. He asked the poor uber driver if he could connect his laptop to the car's sound system to play some music. The driver, though clearly apprehensive, agreed, and within moments, the car was filled with the unmistakable energy of the Red Hot Chili Peppers.

As we drove to the hospital, my head swam with worry, discomfort, and a distinct disbelief. The ride felt like it took an eternity, and with each drumbeat and bassline thumping through the speakers, I became increasingly convinced that my heart was going to give out right there in the backseat. I thought, *what a way to go—with the Chili Peppers providing the soundtrack to my demise.*

Eventually, we arrived at the hospital. Getting out of the Uber and making my way to triage was surreal. My mind raced. What was I going to say? I knew something was terribly wrong, but I couldn't articulate what it was. Was it my heart? Was it something else entirely?

At triage, they didn't waste any time. I was taken straight through, hooked up to a heart monitor, and had bloods drawn. The efficiency was both reassuring and terrifying. They even administered heart medication, which gave me pause—was this really happening? But at that moment, the only thing I cared about was being horizontal again. Lying flat on that hospital bed felt like pure relief after what felt like hours of struggling to stay upright.

Not long after, a doctor came to speak with me. Her expression was calm but serious as she delivered the news: based on my bloodwork, I had experienced a heart attack.

I stared at her in disbelief. Surely, this had to be some kind of mix-up. I told her, half-joking, that she must have confused my results with someone else's. Her response was firm but kind—there was no mistake. I had, without question, suffered a heart attack.

Even as the words hung in the air, I struggled to accept them. A heart attack? Me? It seemed impossible and so implausible. Part of me kept searching for an alternative explanation, something less dramatic, less life threatening. But deep down, I knew I couldn't deny what my body had been trying to tell me all along. This was real, and I couldn't dismiss it any longer.

I could hear the murmurs of doctors nearby, discussing my case. They seemed puzzled. My results didn't align with the usual risk factors for a heart attack—no family history, no smoking, no weight issues, and my age didn't fit the profile either. Their uncertainty added another layer to my own disbelief.

A short while later, a cardiac doctor came to my bedside and asked a simple but profound question: "Have you been under any emotional stress recently?"

Those words opened the floodgates. The dam I had carefully constructed over the past years broke apart, and every raw emotion came rushing back. The grief, the harassment, the relentless stress—it all resurfaced with crushing intensity. I could barely speak, overcome by the weight of everything I had been trying to suppress.

That night, I was transferred to the coronary care unit. The constant beeping of monitors, the soft murmur of hospital staff, and the sterile stillness of the room became my world. Despite the fear and uncertainty, I was profoundly thankful to be lying flat in a place where I felt safe and cared for. Exhausted, I finally drifted off to sleep.

The next morning, my cardiac specialist visited me. With a calm and compassionate tone, he explained his suspicion: I had likely suffered from *Takotsubo Cardiomyopathy*, also known as Broken Heart Syndrome. It was a condition often triggered by intense emotional stress. However, he explained that a formal diagnosis required confirmation through further testing.

An angiogram and an ultrasound followed, and the results were clear—I had Takotsubo Cardiomyopathy. The news was surreal but also oddly validating. My heart hadn't been failing in a conventional sense; it had been literally broken by the weight of years of grief and stress.

After three days in hospital, I was discharged, and I went home with a regimen of cardiac medications. Over the course of a year, my heart began to recover. Follow-up tests, including an ultrasound, bloodwork, and an ECG, showed no lasting damage, except for some tissue scarring. Eventually, I was taken off all my medications and discharged from the care of my cardiologist.

Looking back, I know I am here by the grace of God. It was not my time to go, and I am profoundly thankful for each day I have been given since. I made a conscious decision to approach life with positivity and gratitude. In honour of Richard, I've decided to grab life with both hands, embrace every moment, and live my best life.

But not everything about that hospital stay brings a complete sense of relief. While I was lying in the coronary care unit, vulnerable, scared and alone, an event occurred that still chills me to this day.

The very work colleague who had tormented me for the last five years appeared at my hospital door. He stood there, silent, staring at me, and through me, with an intensity that froze me in place. His presence felt invasive, even menacing. I was paralysed by fear, completely vulnerable, and unsure of his intentions. In that moment, hooked up to monitors and physically weakened, I feared for my life.

Even now, I can't fully explain the terror I felt. It was as though all the pain and harassment he had caused culminated in that single moment, with him standing there, staring through me as if I were nothing more than a target. It is an image I will never forget.

The fact that my colleague didn't work anywhere near the coronary care unit made his presence there even more troubling. When questioned about why he was there, he changed his story four times, each explanation more implausible than the last. That was the breaking point for me. I realised I could no longer tolerate living in fear or wondering what his next move would be. I decided to take out an Apprehended Violence Order (AVO) against him—and I got it.

The sense of relief that came with securing the AVO was immense. It was a formal acknowledgment of his unacceptable behaviour and a step toward reclaiming my peace of mind. While it didn't erase the years of torment, it gave me a renewed sense of control over my life, something I had been missing for far too long.

Love

Chapter Eleven

Lessons

But life after Richard's passing wasn't just marked by dealing with grief and external stressors—it also forced me to confront an entirely different and unexpected challenge: navigating the world of household finances.

Here's the truth, as embarrassing as it is to admit. When Richard died, I had never paid a single bill in my life nor did I know how to. Like many couples, we had divided responsibilities, and financial management was something Richard handled entirely and effectively. I trusted him implicitly to take care of everything, and I had been completely indifferent to any and all of the details.

After his death, I was thrust into a crash course in financial survival. My ignorance wasn't just inconvenient; it was overwhelming. For instance, I wouldn't let anyone turn on the lights for weeks because I had no idea how much electricity cost. I was terrified of running up a bill I couldn't pay. Instead, we relied on candles in the evenings until the next electricity bill arrived and gave me a sense of what we could afford.

The same fear applied to the clothes dryer. I refused to use it, even on the rainiest days, until I saw how much it affected the bill. In the meantime, I went out and bought clothes horses to dry our laundry indoors in front of the fire when it was on. Even then, I waited for them to go on sale, refusing to pay full price. I remember feeling a ridiculous sense of triumph when I snagged two for $12 instead of $15.

It's important to note that Richard had never controlled or restricted our money. He simply managed it, and he did so seamlessly. I had always been grateful to him for taking on that responsibility, especially because I loathed dealing with numbers and spreadsheets. But I didn't realise the extent of his dedication until those final months of his life. Even as his health deteriorated to the point where he couldn't get out of bed, he continued to manage our finances from his bedside. Now, looking back, I appreciate his efforts more than ever.

Embarrassingly enough, I didn't even know how to access our bank accounts. My financial expertise extended only to using our cards or withdrawing cash from an ATM. Beyond that, I was completely lost.

Richard had tried so many times to engage me in learning about our finances. He wanted to show me how everything worked and ensure I had the knowledge to handle things if I ever needed to. But every time, I resisted. Looking back, I realise one of the reasons for my stubbornness—though I never admitted it, even to myself—was that if I didn't know how to manage our finances, then Richard had to. My refusal to learn was my way of holding onto the belief that he would always be there to handle it.

Just after his transplant, Richard sent me a private message from his hospital bed. It was a list of everything I needed to know: our bank account details, passwords, life insurance, superannuation, other insurances, and the deeds to the house. It wasn't the first time he had written this information down for me, but every time before, I had dismissed it. I either ignored it completely or threw it out, convinced I wouldn't ever need it.

This time, I wanted to do the same. The moment I read the message, I wanted to delete it immediately, but this time I thought, *I'll delete this as soon as he gets home.* Perhaps deep down, I knew I shouldn't and couldn't delete this one this time.

I never deleted that message.

Nine months after Richard passed away, I was still waiting for his life insurance payout. By this point, my financial situation was becoming increasingly strained. The bare minimum correspondence I had received from the insurance company was confusing and vague, and in my naivety, I didn't realise it was my responsibility to follow it up constantly. I thought these things just *happened* automatically.

Finally, desperation pushed me to act. I called the insurance company, and with tears of frustration, I asked, "How do you know my children and I aren't living in the gutter? Why is this taking so long?"

The answer I received time and time again left me speechless: Richard's policy was 'under advisement'.

I had no idea what that even meant, but the words filled me with dread. The uncertainty, the lack of communication, and the sheer injustice of the situation were overwhelming. Here I was, nine months into navigating life as a widow, raising my children, learning to manage finances, and trying to keep us afloat—and now I had to fight for something that should have been straightforward.

That phone call marked a turning point. I realised I couldn't afford to be passive any longer, not in my finances, not in my dealings with companies, and certainly not in advocating for my family. I began chasing up the life insurance claim relentlessly, making calls, sending emails, and demanding updates. It was exhausting, but I refused to give up.

Not long after a million frustrating phone calls, the cheque finally arrived in the mail. I didn't pay much attention to it, assuming that the ordeal with the insurance company was finally over. I went straight to the bank to deposit it into my account. The bank staff knew me well by this point; they had heard my story and had always treated me with genuine empathy and kindness.

As the teller processed the cheque, I noticed her expression change. She paused, looked up at me with tears in her eyes, and said, "I'm so sorry, but I can't transfer this cheque into your account."

For a moment, I was stunned. What now? She gently explained that the cheque had been made out to Richard, not me.

Richard.

My heart sank. After everything I'd been through—the months of waiting, the endless phone calls, the emotional exhaustion—this felt like yet another blow I couldn't bear. The teller, as kind as she was, could only do so much. She suggested I go home, contact the insurance company, and request a reissued cheque in my name. She also promised to escalate the issue with her head office.

I went home, tears streaming down my face, and called the insurance company. I explained the situation as calmly as I could, trying to understand why a cheque for Richard's life insurance policy—the one I was listed as the 100% beneficiary of—had been made out to him.

The man on the other end of the phone was dismissive and arrogant, making an already painful situation even worse. "The cheque was made out to Richard because he was the one who took out the policy," he said, his tone dripping with condescension.

I tried to explain that Richard was no longer here, that I was the rightful beneficiary, and that this simple oversight was causing undue stress. He interrupted me, repeating, "Yes, but he was the one who took out the policy."

It was like talking to a brick wall. No matter how much I pleaded or reasoned, they refused to reissue the cheque. I hung up the phone, devastated and overwhelmed, wondering why everything had to be so difficult and hard.

I called the bank again, sobbing as I recounted the conversation. The staff there were a lifeline of compassion in what felt like an endless sea of bureaucracy. After consulting with their head office, they came up with a solution: if I could bring in five forms of identification for Richard, they could open a temporary bank account in his name.

In a deceased person's name.

It felt surreal, digging through Richard's belongings to find the necessary documents. I was doing everything I could to navigate this unfamiliar terrain while still grieving his loss. Once I had gathered the IDs, the bank opened a deceased estate account in Richard's name, processed the cheque, held it for the standard five-day clearance period, and then transferred the funds into my account. Finally, they closed his temporary account.

This ordeal could have broken me, but it didn't. Instead, it reinforced how much resilience I had gained in those months after Richard's passing.

In the midst of this chaos, I often reflected on how fortunate we had been that Richard's career in the police force came with a mandatory life insurance policy. It was a blessing I hadn't fully appreciated until now. When Richard was diagnosed with cancer at 26 years old, he wouldn't have been eligible to take out life insurance on his own. If not for that early, automatic policy, we would have had nothing.

The mandatory policy was a gift of foresight, one that ensured our family's future even when Richard was no longer with us. It's a sobering reminder of the importance of planning for the unthinkable, no matter how invincible we may feel in the moment.

Looking back, I realise how vulnerable and exposed I was during that time. It was as though, in the midst of my grief and confusion, predatory debt collectors could sense an opportunity. They capitalised on the probate process being public knowledge, knowing full well that many people in my position would not have the knowledge or resources to fight back.

The distress they caused was not just financial. It was emotional and psychological. I vividly remember the anguish it brought my children when they would answer the phone and were confronted with someone asking to speak to Richard. Watching them try to process why someone would call for their dad, knowing he was gone, was heartbreaking. I wanted to shield them from everything, but I could not stop the phone from ringing or the letters from arriving.

The sheer audacity of these claims was staggering. While the events they referenced had a kernel of truth—dates and circumstances that matched things I vaguely remembered—they were far from legitimate. The sums they demanded were inflated, and their tone was increasingly aggressive. The supposed court dates regarding these fraudulent claims were entirely fabricated, but their threatening language, both verbal and written, was designed to wear me down.

When they requested Richard's death certificate, it was the final straw. At first, I panicked, thinking that providing it might resolve the situation. But when I could not find the document and remembered my solicitor had it, I decided to call him for advice.

That phone call was another turning point. As I described the extent of the harassment, my solicitor was alarmed and furious. He immediately recognised the tactics being used as fraudulent and predatory. His reaction shook me—until that moment, I had not fully realised how precarious my situation was.

He explained in no uncertain terms how dangerous it would have been to send Richard's death certificate to these so-called agencies. By doing so, I would have effectively validated their claims, opening the door to an avalanche of similar scams from around the world. What I thought was a simple step to prove my innocence could have made me a target for years to come.

From that moment, my solicitor took over completely. He instructed me to have no further communication with any of the debt collectors and to forward every email, phone call, and letter directly to him. He then involved the police, who handled the situation decisively.

After that, the harassment stopped entirely. The silence was as sudden as it was relieving. What could have spiralled into a never-ending nightmare was halted because of the intervention of someone who understood the system and how to protect me.

Reflecting on this, I am endlessly grateful that I did not have that death certificate in my possession at the time. It felt like divine intervention. That single missing document spared me from further exploitation during an already devastating period of my life.

The experience taught me valuable lessons about the importance of seeking professional advice and trusting those who truly have your best interests at heart. It also highlighted how vulnerable people can be during times of grief and transition, and how crucial it is to have safeguards in place to protect against those who seek to exploit that vulnerability.

I share this story not to highlight my past ignorance but to emphasise the importance of shared financial knowledge in a partnership. It's not uncommon for one person to take on the bulk of financial responsibility, but it's crucial for both partners to have at least a basic understanding of the household's finances. Grief is hard enough without the added stress of financial confusion. If my experience helps even one person avoid the same situation, then it's worth the vulnerability of sharing it.

Richard

Chapter Twelve

Acknowledgements

The grief of suddenly losing Richard, the love of my life, my partner, and the father of our children, was a weight so heavy that, at times, it felt as though it would crush me, my soul and my world. Yet for the first five years after his passing, I was forced to put that grief on hold, delay it, and suppress it, as circumstances beyond my control demanded every ounce of my strength and focus. Those years were marked by a pain so deep and complex that it defies simple explanation.

During those five years, there was no space for healing, no opportunity to process the immense loss, and no pathway in finding closure. The constant demands of my reality pushed me into emotional depths I had never known and tested every fibre of my being. Yet, through it all, I clung to the hope that my actions and those of the absolutely incredible and amazing people who I was privileged enough to have stand by me, would not only see us through but also pave the way to protect other families from enduring what we had been through.

One of those remarkable people was Chris, a dear friend of Richard's and mine, who, along with his supportive wife, Linda, became an unshakable source of strength for my children and me. Chris walked this harrowing path with us, carrying some of the emotional burden on his shoulders when I could no longer bear it alone. To this day, I remain profoundly grateful for their compassion and selflessness. I could not have navigated those years without them.

Now, 12 years on, the storm has subsided, though its echoes will always linger. Writing this book has been an incredibly challenging process, stirring memories and emotions I thought I had neatly packed away. Yet it has also been profoundly healing, granting me a sense of peace and closure that my heart and soul has long yearned for.

We would never have chosen this path. None of us would willingly embark on a journey of such pain and loss. But faced with no choice, we have forged ahead, emerging stronger and closer than I ever imagined possible. Today, my children and I are happy, healthy, and, for the most part, thriving. We are moving forward, not as a way of leaving Richard behind but as a way of honouring him and the love he gave us.

In the beginning, I needed constant reminders from my family and friends that Richard would want this for us. I resisted it, clinging to the past, fearing that moving forward would somehow diminish his memory. But now, my heart and soul remind me on their own. I know, without a doubt, that Richard's greatest wish would have been for us to find joy, be happy, to live life fully, and to carry him with us in our hearts as we do.

I have stumbled along the way. I am only human. There were moments when I felt so lost, unsure of which direction to take, and many times when I made mistakes. Grief has a way of turning you upside down, inside out and back to front, disorienting your heart and soul until you no longer know which way is up. But despite it all, I have found my footing and so have our children.

I am proud of myself and the person I have had no choice but to become. Through all of the pain and adversity, I've learned to rise up, and today, I stand strong, confident, generous, and kind. I've learned the importance of backing myself, and my heart is full of love for all of my family and friends. I'm also, just quietly, the Queen of my Castle!

I look at my children, and my heart swells with pride. They have become such incredible people, and I know Richard would be beyond proud of them, just as I am. Emily has completed her policing degree and is now working with a branch of DCJ. She also has a wonderful fiancé, Tom, who has become an important part of our lives. They are getting married in November this year, and I will be the proudest Mother of the Bride! Nicholas is married to beautiful Taylor, and they have 3 beautiful children—Nea, who is three, Grayson, who is one and a baby Desmond born February 12. Nicholas has worked hard, completing his landscaping apprenticeship, and now he's pursuing a degree in theology. Zach, now 22, he's finished his apprenticeship in interior and exterior painting. He's living out of home, near the beach, with friends, and is truly embracing his independence.

Zach, endearingly known as Moonpie, always insists he's the favourite, Emily and Nicholas would agree. But truth be told, he's not, there's no favourite! They are each so unique and bring their own light to our family. I am endlessly proud of the adults they have become, and their growth has been a testament to the strength and resilience they have inherited from both Richard and me.

Richard had a monumental impact on all of us—on me, our children, our family, and our friends. I am certain that his legacy, life, and love will continue to live on in each of us. He touched so many lives with his strength, his unwavering loyalty, his faith, and his love. His presence may no longer be with us physically, but in every memory, every smile, and every shared moment, his spirit remains.

I am fiercely proud, honoured, and privileged to have met, known, loved, married, been blessed with our children, and done life with Richard. Our journey together was nothing short of extraordinary, and even though he is no longer here, his love continues to guide me with every step I take.

I love you, Richard, with all my heart, and I will always love you until the end of time. You were my everything, and you always will be. Thank you for the beautiful life we shared and for the incredible family we built together. You will forever be missed, but you will never be forgotten.

Your wings were ready, but my heart was not.

Richard and Claire

Chapter Thirteen

My Favourite Books & Quotes

BOOKS

A Fortunate Life by AB Facey

Despite all and everything we have been through, I still consider myself to have had, like AB Facey, 'A Fortunate Life.'

The Happiest Man on Earth by Eddie Jak

This book resonated and inspired me. Like Eddie wrote, after having gone through everything he had, he still chose to be happy, to always find the good in people and show kindness to everyone - family, friends, acquaintances and strangers.

I choose this too!

The Light We Carry by Michelle Obama

This book is so true and beautifully uplifting. Uplift those that are in your life – 'Go High.' Always take the high road and don't lower your standards, or who you really are, or what you believe in.

QUOTES

Don't regret growing old, it's a privilege denied to many.
Mark Twain

Never say never.
Charles Dickens

The grass is always greenest where you water it.
Originating from the Greek Poet Ovid

ABOUT THE AUTHOR

After the sudden loss of her husband at 47yrs old, Claire Bodle's grief journey and eventual healing process has inspired her to write this book.

Claire has 3 children and 2 grandchildren, immense and ever grateful for the love of her supportive family and friends, thankful for the strength and courage she has found in her faith, Claire's happy place is being at the beach, swimming in the ocean and consuming a really good coffee.

Working all her adult life as a Surgical Registered Nurse and married for 21yrs, ***I Will Be Your Voice*** is Claire's first book and has been written with the hope that by telling her story, she will give comfort, hope and support to those who read it.

www.ingramcontent.com/pod-product-compliance
Lightning Source LLC
Chambersburg PA
CBHW061736070526
44585CB00024B/2694